Drones

This book is an everything-included approach to understanding drones, creating an organization around using unmanned aircraft, and outlining the process of safety to protect that program. It is the first-of-a-kind safety-focused text book for unmanned aircraft operations, providing the reader with a required understanding of hazard identification, risk analysis, mitigation, and promotion. It enables the reader to speak the same language as any civil aviation authority, and gives them the toolset to create a safety risk management program for unmanned aircraft.

The main items in this book break down into three categories. The first approach is understanding how the drone landscape has evolved over the last 40 years. From understanding the military components of UAS to the standards and regulations evolution, the reader garners a keen understanding of where we came from and why it matters for moving forward. The second approach is in understanding how safety risk management in aviation can be applied to drones, and how that fits into the regulatory and legislative environment internationally. Lastly, a brief synopsis of the community landscape for unmanned aircraft is outlined with interviews from important leaders and stakeholders in the marketplace.

Drones fills a gap in resources within the unmanned aircraft world. It provides a robust understanding of drones, while giving the tools necessary to apply for a certificate of authorization, enabling more advanced flight operations for any company, and developing safety risk management tools for students and career professionals. It will be a mainstay in all safety program courses and will be a required tool for any and all individuals looking to operate safely and successfully in the United States.

Harrison G. Wolf has been on the cutting edge of unmanned aircraft system safety development since 2010. He created the University of Southern California's Safety Management Systems for Remotely Piloted Aircraft Course and is the President of an internationally recognized consulting company, Wolf UAS LLC. Harrison continues to teach at the University of Southern California, USA and provide leadership in the robotics sector.

Drones

Safety Risk Management for the
Next Evolution of Flight

Harrison G. Wolf

Routledge
Taylor & Francis Group

LONDON AND NEW YORK

First published 2017
by Routledge
2 Park Square, Milton Park, Abingdon, Oxon OX14 4RN

and by Routledge
52 Vanderbilt Avenue, New York, NY 10017

First issued in paperback 2020

Routledge is an imprint of the Taylor & Francis Group, an informa business

British Library Cataloguing in Publication Data
A catalogue record for this book is available from the British Library

Library of Congress Cataloging in Publication Data
A catalog record for this book has been requested

ISBN 13: 978−0−367−66989−8 (pbk)
ISBN 13: 978−1−138−20355−6 (hbk)

Typeset in Bembo
by Florence Production Ltd, Stoodleigh, Devon

Contents

Figures

Tables

Introduction

My name is Harrison Wolf. I fly Small Unmanned Aircraft Systems (sUAS) and had an early Section 333 Exemption. I'm a licensed Part 107 Remote Pilot in Command (RPIC) for Unmanned Aircraft. For those of you that know what these are, I commend you and for those that don't, that's just fine. We'll cover them in the following chapters. For now, understand that it means I can fly drones commercially while the Federal Aviation Administration (FAA) finalizes rules and regulations for further commercial use. I also teach at the University of Southern California's Aviation Safety & Security Program and I have written this book to provide the guidance, insight, and understanding of UAS that has allowed me to be successful in the field. I agree with the adage, albeit cliché, that the essence of life is change. Throughout this book you will see change. Whether it is what industry leaders have decided to call UAS or a decision to regulate where in the past no regulations existed, that change is fundamental to the overall well-being of the industry, pilots, operators, manufacturers, the public, and consumers. It is this change that demands differentiation between the drones of war and the drones of commerce. It is change that allows unmanned systems to cultivate better crops or find a missing child. It is dynamism and the entrepreneurial spirit which promote exponential growth of the flying robots subject to this book. While this change is a wondrous thing which allows for old and new problems to be solved by innovative college students or wartime veterans, it also brings difficult new problems that must be overcome before dreams can be realized. Drones offer the promise of providing a bird's eye view to all people with little training, at low cost, and for the benefit of the planet, people, and animals. It is up to how we deal with change to understand the true potential of unmanned aircraft.

When I think upon where the unmanned aircraft integration effort is, I smile when others frown. Alarmists are quick to tear down the FAA's "lack of speed." They do hold some valid points about *waiting too long to act* and are rightfully scared about the potential for overbearing regulation for commercial operations. Hobbyists are likewise scared that their activity—often passed on from a loving father or mother—is at risk for overregulation having had the Sauron-like eye of government cast upon them. No, I smile because I see the success of UAS in the success of railroads and airplanes, and see that though we are just beginning down a long road to full and seamless integration, we have set upon a path well-trodden by previous technologies. There is an old saying amongst those in the public policy field—one of my many backgrounds—that it takes the goldilocks approach to regulatory developments before we truly support an industry appropriately. First we under regulate, then we overregulate, and finally we regulate just the right amount. This book is being written at a time when regulations are changing rapidly and there is a good chance that once it is published the environment will have changed. This is okay as, though the regulations themselves may change, the evolving approach to how to develop and understand the industry continues in one direction. Performance-based regulations and a reliability-based approach that requires risk assessment and a solid understanding of an operation are undeniably the future of UAS regulations and standards. You can rest assured that though the laws evolve, the way we develop standards, regulations, and thus consider technology will not. The foundation for how industry is integrated with government, and how government considers the theoretical impact on society, will remain roughly the same.

Imagine for a moment seeing the eventual capability of a steam engine just as it is being shown to the public. You didn't invent it, yet you feel kinship and ownership over it as the inspiration of wonder thrills through your body and overwhelms your soul. What could you do with such a thing? You could move men across nations, move food to drought-stricken places. You could devastate armies and win wars with an ironclad ship, a faster railroad with greater constitution, or provide endless power for new mechanized

Figure 0.1 Drone with professional cinema camera flying over summer park
    © Alexey Yuzhakov

weaponry. You could save lives, grow commerce, or close the gap from coast to coast. There are, of course, challenges before you do that. You must create signals and communications lines. You need to buy up land routes and acquire steel. You must build track and protect that track; personnel for safety and security are required. It isn't enough to simply discover and invent something new. There is an entire support structure that, to be successful, requires whole communities of participants. This is the stage where we find UAS. Drones have had so much wartime success that the US Air Force is calling its latest fighter project its last manned fighter. We must now build the communities of knowledge and safety to ensure the success and well-being for all. We must educate the public to reduce the fear and promote the benefits, be they environmental, commercial, artistic, or personal.

Introducing new technologies for public use is a daunting task. It requires a continued cooperation between industry leaders, government regulators, and the "don't tell me what to do, just let me do it" public operators who are—ultimately—the most important determinant for the success of the system. The modern world seeks freedom from authority, access to immediate relief in the most dire disasters, and feelings of wonder in the combination of art and technology. Global populations are experiencing economic freedom, political freedom, and equality that demand much, but reward even more, some for the first time. Unfortunately, the forces of safety and industry promotion and protection come to a head with the speed of innovation and the desires of the market. In these circumstances, the pathway forward can be difficult—riddled with "cease and desist" letters, fines for inappropriate use, and legal actions that no one really wants—not the operators, not the regulators, not the courts.

While the purpose of this book is to educate and provide information and background to the operators of the future, its equally important goal is to get everyone to speak the same language on the domestic and international front. If an applicant in the UK speaks the same language as the UK Civil Aviation Authority—providing the documents, training, certifications, and knowledge that they expect—the applicant will have a much easier time understanding the meaning behind rules, and the aviation authority will find it easy to grant approval for their operation. If a drone manufacturer in the United States is seeking a Type Certification for their drone, knowing the Type Certification process as well as the risk assessment and Concept of Operations (CONOPs) process will reduce the time it takes and the overall success of their venture. It's important that we all understand how to talk to one another on the ground, in the air, and through documentation.

I often speak to FAA regulators and international standards developers about unmanned aircraft systems at conferences, in teleconferences or video-conferences, and through email. To me, they are not some Wizard of Oz figure, behind a curtain, making decrees without deference to the struggle or mission of the everyday operator or hobbyist. Those who work for regulatory bodies, or who help create the standards by which the industry is formed, are not faceless bureaucrats who would like nothing more than to shut down this nascent technology. These regulators are people who, more than likely, have a drone that they fly with their families or friends and want to create an environment of safety within collaboration, and provide meaningful, but adaptive, frameworks for flight. Most, I kid you not, love to fly drones as a hobby and have manned aviation experience themselves. They love this stuff just as much as you and I.

It is very important to understand the international environment for flight, as the world moves together toward a safe, integrated international airspace. There are many similarities between the United States and other nations endeavoring to bring together manned aviation with unmanned aviation. There is also dissimilarity between even heavily standardized national airspaces all party to International Civil Aviation Organization (ICAO) standards and guidance. While nation states are all moving toward the same goal, each has interests that must be met, and characteristics that reflect differences in approach. European civil aviation is much less diverse than the United States, and the airspace works very differently. Some nations have highly regulated airspace where civil aviation is minimal (Europe, France, Netherlands, Russia) and there are others where civil aviation is much more present (United States, Australia).

Differences in airspace management techniques, operational approaches, cultural biases and bureaucratic systems all require political support, and it is no surprise that individual countries approach the integration of unmanned aircraft systems differently, even with the same goal of integration and safety. In Australia, for example, regulators have seen fit to authorize union heads with an ability to authorize missions in the national airspace, as has New Zealand, while South Africa has rescinded their open airspace, once recognized as a leader in "freedom of flight" for sUAS operations. While the Minister of Transportation, Poppy Khoza, signed new guidelines for operating locations, operators and manufacturers still see the regulatory environment as "more difficult and more constrictive." Meanwhile, throughout Africa, ICAO is being admonished for not acting quickly enough to publish guidelines for UAS and the South African Civil Aviation Authority (SACAA), as seen by Khoza's comment that "In the absence of guiding documents from ICAO, regulators such as ourselves have had to swiftly derive measures to address the regulation deficiency in response to a growing demand to regulate this sector" (Khoza 2015). The FAA and other civil aviation authorities (CAAs) have all been called to action in a similar way, and the belief that the technology is adapting quicker than the regulators can regulate defines the UAS community.

A technology that poses little risk to the public can often become a practical, useful, well-integrated component of any national system within a matter of years. When new technologies mature in an environment of paranoia, political wrangling, and a misunderstanding of the fundamental application for use, however, it can be nearly impossible for it to be successfully embraced by the public. In these situations, federal governments not only have the role of developing regulations by which the new technology is policed, in this case unmanned aerial systems (UAS), they must also become the proponent and cheerleader of such emerging systems; finding it necessary to assure the public that the technology will be handled and introduced safely, timely, and with an overall positive impact. Until recently, the terms "Dirty, Dangerous, and Dull" had been used for unmanned aircraft missions throughout every stakeholder presentation as characterizations for where UAS can be best applied. Largely, this quick-and-easy terminology and definition comes from the military applications of UAS overseas—what they see as a technology that should be used for the dirty missions, the dangerous missions, and the dull missions. Recently, this has changed as commercial promoters find footholds among farmers, miners, photographers, Hollywood, and many others. The "Triple D" of UAS still does come up and it really is setting back the industry. If we continue to think of UAS as having a specific role for minimal applications, we won't understand the true implication of automated flight. We will undoubtedly miss applications and approaches for UAS that can revolutionize not only these triple-D missions, but missions beyond the dirty, dangerous or dull environments.

The Dirty, Dangerous, and Dull mantra espoused by operators in the field works for them, but it is not in any way winning the war at home. Some operators are in fact filling crucial roles that are defined by the triple-D missions. Military, paramilitary, government researchers, and oil companies use drones for missions that are dirty, dangerous, and dull as they fly over deserts and swamps while seeking African rhino poachers or herds, watch for icebergs over frigid temperatures to protect their pipelines, fly through smoke and debris to monitor volcanic activity, take aerial images of strip mines to look at mineral deposits above and below ground, and reconnoiter over terrorist suspects to ensure a successful military strike. Agricultural pilots from the big boys at Monsanto™ to the small, single farmers in Japan use the same Yamaha™ style RMAX UAS helicopter for dusting crops with pesticide or herbicide, or the newer more agile SenseFly ebee™ for analyzing crop temperatures, monitoring field water tables, and providing security to their borders—dirty and dull if not so dangerous. The dirty, dangerous, and dull mindset that was born as military commanders worked through their post-Cold War era munitions and technology companies made sales pitch after sales pitch to the top brass, simply does not translate to the commercial populous internationally.

In a June 2012 poll of Americans conducted by Monmouth University, it was found that while "an overwhelming majority of Americans support the idea of using drones to help with search and rescue missions . . . and two-thirds of the public also support using drones to track down runaway criminals (67%) and control illegal immigration on the nation's border (64%)," roughly 64% would be "very concerned or concerned" about drone use for domestic applications citing their main concerns as privacy violations (Murray 2012). In a more recent poll, the support of law enforcement use specifically for search and rescue missions grew to 83%, showing a consistent belief that there is a significant use for UAS in the National Air Space System, and that those uses could fit into a national integration that will both protect privacy and accomplish needed missions (Murray 2013). These polls have continued to show that the public is becoming more and more accepting of UAS in the airspace, though privacy is still a major concern for most populations.

It's important to get away from this boring portrayal of what a drone is for militaries, and into the mindset of how the world sees drones, while looking for the next big, great technology to embrace and develop. We are just now seeing the culmination of decades of research and development in robotics, automation, processing, communications, and bandwidth speeds that enable the most amazing applications of technology to a general consumer. This is the precipice of a new generation just as the Civil War was for the steam engine, the First World War was for airplane and automotive, and the Second World War was for mass-production and replaceable parts. The last 20 years of war, from Beirut to Iraq and Afghanistan, brought the widespread, declassified, grunt-level warrior's use of the unmanned aircraft to the forefront of the public's eye. What was once the biggest-held, least-used wartime technology became the most pervasive military poster child for this newest generation of war. While unmanned aircraft technologies have existed for nearly 50 years, they were infantile compared to the capabilities of today's technology systems.

Is it surprising, then, that this same technology—just as the wars begin to wind down and those users return home—continues to grab the mind of the average American? Is it any wonder that this new tech, with a lower cost in all aspects than a standard manned airplane, would become so sought after for applications at home? No, but the mindset must change in how we approach it. As regulators drive on to make the environment safe and secure, we cannot continue to identify it as used only for the most dangerous and dirty jobs. This continual use of dangerous and dirty only reinforces the connection to the way the military treated these drones—expendable, crashable, and cheap (as they are cheap compared to a F-18 or U-2 spy plane) tools to be used up and discarded. We must begin to forge a new understanding; that these should be flown in a safe manner, in a secure method. We must understand that these are not simply tools just as they are not strictly airplanes—they are something in between. They are new technology requiring a safety first approach, and the only way that they will continue to promulgate is through safe, secure regulations, operating in legal ways, with a meaningful understanding of the balance between automation and the human operator.

It is my intention to share through personal relationships, growth, and experience how the international airspace integration efforts for unmanned aircraft systems are moving forward and how any operator can begin to fly using the most advanced safety knowledge theory; cultivated through countless accidents—"written in blood"—that will be required by the Federal Aviation Administration. This book includes interviews conducted with industry leaders and visionaries to get their perspective on how they approach reliability, which operators are developing the newest systems, and how they believe the UAS market will develop. This book includes interviews from those responsible for operations and management in order to show how those responsible for safety and acquiring flight data integrate their daily lessons learned from operators at their facility, in the hopes the reader will better understand how to do the same. Finally, and perhaps most importantly, the book contains interviews with association leaders and community leaders who understand the plight of small, medium, and large UAS operators in order to outline the most important discussions shaping the future of the industry.

It is impossible to move forward in the discussion of UAS without first discussing the immense push from free market forces. Businesses throughout all industries are identifying the potential positive benefits of incorporating unmanned systems into their operations, and entrepreneurs are eyeing the unmanned robotics market expectantly. The UAS industry is growing rapidly and integration into the national airspace is a key element in the development of the NextGen Airspace for the United States.[1] According to the Teal Group, there will be upwards of $91 billion in aggregate spending in the UAS industry over the next decade alone (Teal Group 2014). Perhaps more importantly, the United States could represent 62 per cent of the worldwide research and development for UAS—a significant lead internationally and an important national security component when examining proliferate technologies from a command and control perspective. It is important to note, however, that the Teal Group specifically identified regulatory hold-ups as a fundamental enabler for growth. Without advancement, it is likely that European and Asian companies will dominate the market landscape. Over the past year the FAA has endeavored to keep up with its European counterparts, and yet even so European Aviation Safety Agency (EASA) and the International Civil Aviation Authority have continued their serious pursuit of full integration into their airspaces.

This positive assessment of the market opens an entirely new demand to the supply of UAS and will undoubtedly support a non-military transfer of technology necessary for continued growth. Continued growth is assumed in this book as it is unlikely that the research, innovation, and commercial adoption will diminish. For those of us lucky enough to be involved in the conferences, tradeshows, and business opportunities, we see the impact that UAS is having already. New companies are popping up weekly, offering innovative solutions for problems that until now were too expensive to solve. We're increasing crop yields, reducing ground water pollution, protecting endangered wild life, and all of this is just the beginning.

The assimilation of UAS into the national airspace is a complicated task and it is the goal of this book to introduce the major milestones, goals, and complications currently being encountered as well as how to operate concurrently with the development of that system. It is the intent that this book will help the reader recognize and understand international regulatory frameworks, the FAA regulation roadmap as set forth in the FAA Modernization and Reform Act of 2012, and more recent changes that are perhaps in draft rather than their final form. It may be that regulations change after the

Figure 0.2 Aerial view of Bhumiphol Bridge, Bangkok, Thailand © Stockphoto Mania

publication of this book, but the reader will understand significant approaches that regulatory agencies are taking in developing an international framework for UAS integration, and will have a unique toolset to understand those differences. From a more specific perspective, the responsibility of industry leaders and semi-governmental groups such as EUROCAE, Joint Authorities for Rulemaking of Unmanned Systems (JARUS), RTCA, and ASTM are examined to show the involvement of non-governmental organizations (NGOs) in the regulatory process.

I will be drawing upon my personal experiences with RTCA on the Safety Work Group of Special Committee 203, and as the technical chair for the ASTM F-38.02 Best Practices of Operational Risk Assessments for Unmanned Aircraft (UAS) subcommittee. I hope that these experiences will illuminate the behind-the-scenes standards developments that are ongoing to show that drone regulations are not easy, are not haphazard, and are certainly being thought of respectfully and collaboratively. The next steps in the process for UAS's inclusion into the national airspace are identified and the problems moving forward related to the public, to hazard identification, tolerance levels of risk, and mitigation of incidents and accidents. It should also be noted that much of this book, unless otherwise noted, is the sole opinion of the author and does not represent the opinions of any other organization.

While the regulatory frameworks are very important and highlighted at length within this volume, I am also focusing on the components of drone flight that are necessary for a successful application to the national airspace. While this book is explained as a theoretical and academic effort, it will also encompass information that is necessary when applying for exemptions, approvals, certifications, or operational deviance. The two sections that exemplify this goal discuss a full CONOPs, and full implementation and understanding of a Safety Management System (SMS). These two elements, together, will provide any operator an advantage that is lacking in the drone industry. While many operators do understand that safety is important, and may incorporate checklists, briefings, or even some risk analysis, generally operators without previous commercial flight experience or military background try to cut corners and do not satisfy requirements beyond legal operation. In the safety game, we say "Legal is not necessarily safe," to mean that just because you meet basic requirements does not mean you are as safe as you could be. Safety is not an end goal, but a mission in and of itself, and the sections discussing SMS will highlight how to develop and implement a robust system that makes safety the highest priority. Likewise, the CONOPs section will provide insight into how to understand and approach every operation or system design. It comes directly from my work with ASTM setting best practices for UAS operations and will likely be a core element of the regulatory requirements in the future.

Finally, it is my intent to include stories, biographies, and interviews with some of the leading UAS figures from the industry development of the last decade. These individuals have brought their unique perspective, insights, and leadership to help promote unmanned aircraft flourish through personal involvement and industry acceptance. These interviews should highlight the future of unmanned aircraft systems, how the past has led to the present in the industry, and why they are excited about the future. If I have done my job well, this should help you, the reader, understand the diversity and depth that defines this unique marketplace and allow you better understanding of how the community has evolved, where in the community you would like to focus, and what opportunities will exist moving forward.

I hope to share my strong passion for the unmanned aircraft industry and to create a robust and deep knowledge of how UAS operations are made safer and more secure, while maintaining the mystique that exudes from each connection of every robot. Robotics, simply put, is intriguing and inspiring, and it is our job to develop an industry that is safe and secure even while operating in the most diverse operational environments.

1 A quick history of drones

Unmanned aerial systems are new for civil aviation; however, they are nothing new to the military aficionado or warrior who in some form or another has been around drones for quite a while. While there has been a recent shift of support for unmanned aircraft in military organizations, the systems have been developing for over 60 years—some say over a century[2]—and gone through many mission profiles. Only recently has a focus on unmanned aircraft been an accepted part of the military culture, where pilots were pilots, not sitting in a chair thousands of miles from the action. Understanding where these systems came from and how they were integrated into the military ranks sheds light on both problems faced moving forward as well as possible solutions to problems encountered stateside. This history is not intended to be an exhaustive survey of Unmanned Aircraft Vehicle (UAV) history over the last century, but instead included to familiarize the reader with the progression of domestic UAVs. Every month, there is a Cold War era program introduced to me which I had not encountered previously.

The beginning of the modern UAV could be seen in a speech given in 1956 by Air Force Major General David Baker, addressing a meeting of industry and military leaders as, "We can readily see that except for certain types of missions, the manned combat aircraft will become technically obsolete in the future" (Erhard 2010: 4). While his comments addressed the new role of the intercontinental ballistic missile development and use, the backdrop included "sophisticated, jet-powered target drones . . . [and] . . . camera-carrying derivatives of jet drones operated by Air Force pilots . . ." that would soon be the first combat UAV in history (Erhard 2010: 5). While the development of UAVs started early, the systems did not become well supported in the Air Force as they faced "independent externalities" such as internal-political threat, cultural backlash, and basic technological hindrances in the form of location detection, targeting difficulties, and training. Simply put, the vision and foresight existed beyond the capability of the machine.

The greatest contributor in the United States, and perhaps the world, to the continued development of the UAV has been the US intelligence community—specifically the National Reconnaissance Office (NRO) and the CIA (Central Intelligence Agency). Between 1960 and 2000 the "intelligence

Figure 1.1 A BQM-34 Firebee II drone is carried aloft under the wing of NASA's B-52 mothership during a 1977 research flight © NASA

community budget funded roughly 40% of the total US UAV investment, double that of the next greater contributor." Though funded by clandestine organizations, the Air Force was responsible for partial funding and complete operation of each UAV developed during this time. The first, large push for combat drones came from "off budget" projects picked up by the US Air Force originally solicited by the NRO for use with aerial surveillance over communist nations. These programs would be run throughout the 1960s and into the 1970s and they are often referred to as the original NRO "Program D" projects.

In mid-April 1960, Ryan Aeronautical presented the Air Staff with a proposal for a strategic reconnaissance drone—the first of its kind as an alternative to risky U-2 over flights. The Soviet Union had recently developed the SA-2 surface-to-air missile capable of shooting down a U-2 spy plane. Two weeks after this meeting, on May Day, 1960, an American U-2 was shot down over Soviet territory—the plane and pilot were captured, and the pilot tried in an internationally publicized court trial. This was the catalyst that the UAV industry needed to cultivate demand for an unmanned spy plane variant. In response, a contract was signed for the development of "Red Wagon" Unmanned Aircraft Vehicle while a similar, if not bigger and more ambitious UAV, code named "Oxcart," was also being developed by the CIA. Oxcart would eventually be dubbed the A-12 and finally renamed the SR-71 Blackbird. That's right, the same SR-71 that has become ubiquitous with Cold War era technology development was initially intended to be a drone (McIninch 1994).

Though Red Wagon had the support of General Curtis LeMay and Secretary of Defense Roswell Gilpatrick, Harold Brown, Director of Defense Research and Engineering, vetoed the project; diverting all funds to project Oxcart in early 1960—$96 million in total. While the shooting down of this U-2 had the effect of increasing interest in UAV development, it also increased the drive for satellite imagery, communication, and surveillance. These would in the short-term limit mission roles and funding for UAVs, but in the long term enable new unmanned systems to thrive as they would become GPS guided, using satellite communications and imagery for all applications. It should also be noted that mission roles and responsibilities are still in changing balances between these three modes of strategic reconnaissance—drones, satellites, and manned aircraft. If we were to look at the current military roles of these three systems, we would see that they are, or in most cases intended to be, fully integrated components of one larger combat group. This was not the case until recently, and the roles remained unbalanced, and thought of as interchangeable.

The National Reconnaissance Offices' public image for their office "Program D," entitled Big Safari, continued throughout the 1960s to run "low-rate modifications" to manned aircraft. Among these programs the RB-50E/G Haystack, C-130 Rivet Victor, and Ryan Q-2C are the most significant; the Ryan Q-2C Firebee, Model 147A Firebee target drone, becoming the main targeting drone used by the Air Force during this time (Erhard 2010: 6). The Firebee is notable for its place in history as one of two explanations for the term "drone." Some historians believe that the term drone came from reference to the "Fire Bee" specifically since the male workers of the bee hive are drones, while others believe that, like a drone, the unmanned aircraft system is controlled without a mind of its own.

The most notable use of the Firebee never took place. On October 14, 1962, U-2 spy planes tasked with maintaining visual surveillance of Cuba, passed over a lightly clouded coastline taking aerial images for later analysis and what they discovered were newly built nuclear missile installations in Cuba. The US reacted, going on 72-hour operational alert (Erhard 2010: 8). The United States Air Force was set into motion and a variety of missions were drawn to increase surveillance, protect American lives, and move towards nuclear targeting. The Firebee was set to be deployed over Cuba using state-of-the-art camera imaging, loaded on a GC-130 mother ship. At this time, the main configuration for any Firebee launch was by being loaded under the wings of a military cargo plane. When some distance from the target was reached, the Firebee would be dropped from the payload clip and initiate firing of its rocket engine. Over the next eight hours the GC-130 sat ready to take off on the runway. The Firebee had never been used up until this point as an offensive imaging solution to a need for unmanned surveillance. Understanding that this new technology would change how imagery was taken, and then again, countered by enemy forces, Secretary LeMay called to kill the flight, as he wanted to protect the technology's secrecy for flights over mainland Soviet nations. Lloyd Ryan, then an Air Force colonel and drone proponent, recalled in a given interview in December 2008, "We only had two, and we had great visions of greater potential elsewhere [over the Soviet Union] . . . Le May flat out told the undersecretary, not only, 'No,' but 'Hell, no'" (Erhard 2010: 8).

It would be quite some time before UAVs would have an opportunity to prove their use. The Firebee would soon be renamed Lightning Bug in March, 1963, as the top secret program name had been compromised.

The Lightning Bug would become the main platform adopted by the Air Force until 1972, adopting a great many varieties for operations in Vietnam. Most interesting and important of these variations was the 147TE Combat Dawn SIGINT version deployed to Osan Air Base, Korea, with a more powerful engine, real-time data link, and an NSA (National Security Agency) package. These UAVs collected radar data from targets in North Korea at very high altitude. The emergence of satellites for communications, reconnaissance, and data transfer led to the demise of most UAV development and operation as satellites could boast real-time digital image processing. In a "watershed decision," the NRO transferred its entire SR-71, U-2, and drone inventory to the Air Force in 1974 as the NRO had become focused entirely on satellites by 1974; essentially outsourcing its airborne reconnaissance to the Air Force. It would not be until new dangers from the Soviet Union emerged that the reconnaissance UAV would find new life; dangers requiring a solution other than episodic satellite coverage. The mid-1970s provided for the advent of the microprocessor which led to a "meteoric rise" in sophisticated communications

Dryden Flight Research Center ECN-3804 Photographed 1973
F-15 Remotely Piloted Research Vehicle mounted
under the wing of NASA's B-52. NASA photo
Historic Photographs / Historische Fotografien   V like Vintage

Figure 1.2 F-15 remotely piloted aircraft research vehicle (RPRV) mounted under wing of NASA's B-52 © NASA

and sensor electronics allowing for new UAV technologies—stealth aircraft design, digital fly-by-wire autopilots, composite structures, and Global Positioning System satellites all contributed to innovation for UAV mission and design. With these advances, a newly refreshed perception of threat from the Soviet Union, and a new presidential administration friendly to arms budgeting all contributed to the creation of the Advanced Airborne Reconnaissance System (AARS).

As Ronald Reagan became President upon promises to restore military strength in 1980, the transition team for intelligence identified airborne surveillance as a "perceived shortfall." Soon after, $1.5 billion per year was granted to the NRO budget for the development of "long-endurance (up to two days), high altitude reconnaissance aircraft . . . [with] . . . remotely piloted vehicles (RPVs), possibly stealth technology . . ." and that they, ". . . should be reviewed for . . . strategic intelligence collection" (Erhard 2010: 14). The UAV industry received an influx in funding at this point as mission stratagem centered upon "commonality" vendoring originally developed for an ill-fated joint-strike fighter concept from the 1960s (Erhard 2010: 14). With a focus on "commonality," a Joint UAV experiment under the leadership of the UAV Joint Program Office (JPO) began development between the Navy and Air Force; this experiment was tasked with developing a medium-range UAV (MR-UAV)—essentially a jet-powered, compact, alternative to the Lightning Bug useful in tactical reconnaissance support air operations with data-linkage. This aircraft—BQM-145A—received a new, unique mission profile in that it required a modular payload with "joint" tasks allocations to be placed alongside manned aircraft: F-16Rs (Erhard 2010: 15). This would be the first time that both manned and unmanned platforms were intended to be used in conjunction, taking advantage of benefits for both. The BQM-145A would eventually suffer from a "one size fits all" mentality in design in order to satisfy the misconception that *jointness* in operations and system design were necessary for success and continued use. However, a first step in the process of integrating UAVs with manned systems had been taken and would continue even after the project was cancelled.

The UAV Joint Program Office (JPO) had failed to live up to the role it was challenged with as MR-UAV BQM-145A—the joint, manned/ unmanned interfacing system was underutilized and never saw meaningful operation with a blossoming budget increase of 300% from previous predictions ($3.5 billion). As the UAV JPO began to dwindle programs and shutter obsolete initiatives, a few programs moved to the Defense Airborne Reconnaissance Office (DARO) where, while no new UAV programs were fielded in its tenure, budgetary allotments were given to highly successful UAVs of Israeli-influenced design—Pioneer, MQ-1 Predator, MQ-9 Predator, and Global Hawk. Short-range UAV Hunter and medium-range Pioneer and Predator were developed with relationships between TRW, General Atomics, DARO, and Defense Airborne Reconnaissance Program (DARP). Funding for highly specialized micro-UAVs, medium-ranged UAVs, high-altitude UAVs, and special tactical

UAVs is increasing dramatically and now the Air Force, Army, Navy, Coast Guard, National Guard deployed in Iraq, and Marines all incorporate a wide variety of unmanned aerial systems in their operations. This trend only continues to increase.

Case study: NASA's unmanned organizational flaws

Unmanned aircraft capture our attention for reasons that go beyond technology. These amazing aircraft started as military machines; flying robots that soar thousands of feet above the ground delivering a bird's eye account of all that lies below. Others are even more attention-grabbing with a capability to deliver the wrath of nations onto their enemies or provide vaccines for illness-stricken populations during the worst of climactic events. They stealthily hover over sold-out stadiums and international events to sense biological, radiological, or explosive residues to identify threats, prevent casualties, and ensure the public welfare beyond the warzone, and in the assumed sanctuary of urban life. This was not always the case. Unmanned aircraft have gone through near constant evolution over the last century as technological advances changed the very way systems communicate and processes are automated. Hard lessons had to be learned through crashes, and safety considerations developed along with these accidents and mishaps, just as they have with manned aviation. Unlike manned aviation, those crashes often did not take any lives and provided accessible narratives from their pilots.

Those in the aviation industry understand that a mishap or accident is a curse, just as it is a blessing. Lives lost are terrible and any accident in the UAS world that causes damage or the loss of life will set the industry back tremendously. However, if the important lessons of the accident are drawn out, in order to reduce the risk of future faults or mishaps, then that same accident may be a positive turning point for an organization or industry. Such was the case of the F-15 Remotely Piloted Vehicle Program conducted in the late 1960s and early 1970s by the National Aeronautics and Space Administration (NASA). NASA had already been using remotely piloted aircraft to test theory and analytics for design of aircraft, but the newest McDonnell-Douglas F-15 Eagle in development required extensive modeling prior to full performance evaluation and production. As NASA had become known for their use of radio-controlled models for the aerodynamic testing of wingless space-reentry vehicles, they were asked to conduct Air Force modeling prior to final production.

In 1969, the Air Force had recognized the need for a Mach 2-capable jet-powered fighter plane utilizing air superiority and capability lessons learned over the sky of Vietnam. This prototype first flew in 1972, prior to which Major General Benjamin Belli—then Chief of the F-15 System Program Office at Wright-Patterson Air Force Base, Ohio—requested NASA assistance in testing a three-eighths-scale model remotely piloted version (Merlin 2013). The goal of this testing was to identify, configure, and analyze the extremely dangerous maneuvers involving high-angle-of-attack flight and spins. The remotely piloted aspect to test this scale model allowed for limited testing without the use of a test pilot—significantly reducing the overall risk associated with flight testing stall and spin-recovery techniques. The overall contract awarded to McDonnell-Douglas required building three F-15 RPV models for $762,000—or roughly $250,000 per aircraft—a much smaller sum than the usual $6.8 million for a full-scale aircraft (Hallion and Gorn 2003). These models measured 23.5 feet long and consisted largely of fiberglass and wood while weighing roughly 2,500lb. The models had no internal propulsion system and had been designed for a recovery method consisting of a mid-air "catch" by helicopter after deploying a parachute.

This Remotely Piloted Vehicle was unique in that it was built to be dropped. Suspended under the wing of a modified B-52 Stratofortress (much like the Ryan AQM-34 Firebee targeting drone mentioned above), the miniaturized F-15 RPV would be carried to an altitude of 45,000 feet. It would then be released from its "launch pylon" as the aircraft reached 175 knots. On October 12, 1973, the first flight of the F-15 model took place as it was dropped from the B-52 over the Dryden Flight Research Center in Mojave, California. The pilot, Einar Enevoldson, glided the virgin craft for nine minutes without any problems and upon reaching 15,000 feet altitude, a 12-foot spin-recovery parachute deployed in order to stabilize the descent of the aircraft. After the final parachutes had also deployed following the stabilized descent, the aircraft was plucked from the air by a hook suspended by cable from a helicopter and ultimately released onto a cushioned bag on site. The first flight was a success (Reed 1980).

Though the first flight was a success, pilot Einar Enevoldson would go on to pilot many more flights using these models of the F-15 Eagle, and his feedback represents the majority of pilots after they have flown RPVs. In post-flight interviews, Einar admitted that flying the RPV was "both physically and psychologically challenging . . . [and that] a lack of physical cues left him feeling detached from the essential reassuring sensations of flight that ordinarily provide a pilot with situational feedback." When the team would go on to re-enact the same flight in a simulator, they found that the feeling in the simulator was slower than the actual flight by a factor of 1.5 (Dana 1973). Further, as the pilot's heart rate was monitored, it was found that though the usual heart rate for a test flight for this pilot was between 70 and 80 beats per minute, Enevoldson's ranged from 130 to 140 beats per minute reflecting increased stress load, discomfort, and adrenaline.

In later flight Enevoldson and other pilots explored control and stability characteristics of the F-15 models which led to officials at the F-15 Joint Test Force to move forward with piloted spin trials at Edwards Air Force Base. Another pilot, Bill Dana, confirmed that the speed of flight felt about "1.4 times" the actual speed when training in real-time simulation and that once the simulator had been sped up to 1.4 times real-time, it gave a much more "realistic experience." Interestingly, during a post-flight debrief, Dana was asked how he enjoyed flying the RPV. His reply was that the experience was

> quite different from sitting in a cockpit of an actual vehicle, where he generally worried and fretted until just before launch . . . then he could settle down and just fly the plane. With the RPV, he said he was calm and cool until launch and then felt keyed up through recovery.

The same debrief and feelings are often described in nearly all unmanned flights in which the pilot has previous manned aircraft experience. This is something the industry is working tirelessly to alleviate as increased workload stress directly influences fatigue and is one of the most important factors leading to mishaps and accidents. In tests run at the University of Southern California's Aviation Safety & Security Program, very experienced pilots likewise reported feeling "extremely stressed," "exhausted," and "anxious" when simply managing a UAS operation through a pilot.

Remotely piloted aircraft (RPAs) often have unique methods for take-off or landing as this case points out. As introduced earlier, in order to "land,"

NASA Dryden Flight Research Center Photo Collection
http://www.dfrc.nasa.gov/gallery/photo/index.html
NASA Photo: ECN-4891   Date: 1975

F-15 RPRV landing on lakebed

Figure 1.3 F-15 RPRV landing on lakebed at NASA Dryden (1975) © NASA

the F-15 model was expected to release three separate parachutes: the first to stabilize the descent of the vehicle and the final two to offer a significant area to "catch" the craft by helicopter. This system led directly to two mishaps relating to the "catch." Success of this phase of flight required functioning of the three parachutes in conjunction with a parachute release mechanism that enabled the parachute to separate from the aircraft and then the model winched up to a ferry position under the helicopter. On July 10, 1974, the first of several mishaps involving the mid-air recovery system (MARS) parachute recovering occurred during the ninth flight of the model.

During the ninth flight of operation all systems were go for pilot Enevoldson to activate the recovery parachute system. After performing the requisite maneuvers and obtaining stability control data, Einar initiated the recovery parachute system. Everything worked perfectly until the main parachute failed to separate after being "caught" by the helicopter capture cable. This parachute continued to produce strong drag forces and started outlining winch drum cable at an alarming rate. The helicopter crew, acting quickly, attempted to force the main chute separation by breaking the line from the winch drum— much like holding fast to a running large fish will break a fisherman's line. The F-15 RPV landed with the main parachute and 400 feet of load line trailing behind it, on the Edwards Precision Impact Range Area (PIRA). This flight ended with the airframe being dragged nearly a quarter of a mile, dragged by the unseparated parachute sail.

Figure 1.4 DAST-2, a modified BQM-34 Firebee II drone, undergoes calibration in a hangar at the NASA Dryden Flight Research Center © NASA

What was the cause? An investigation that followed found that human error had been the main contributor to this accident (Merlin 2013: 14). Through investigation and root cause analysis of the accident, it was discovered that the crew chief had improperly assembled the parachute release mechanism with a further failure of an inspector to catch the error prior to the flight. Other factors were identified that contributed to that accident, including faulty design by the manufacturer which allowed the incorrect installation of the mechanism, and poor documentation of procedures for installing the mechanism as they had been spread over multiple documents rather than just one document. Compounding these latent failures were that the regular inspector had been out ill and the usual mechanic had been replaced by a mechanic unfamiliar with the parachute system. Investigators continued in their report acknowledging that "Air Force MARS crew had previously experienced an identical incident, but that they had not shared this data with F-15 RPRV project personnel."

Investigators began to unravel further organizational flaws that had become endemic to NASA and flight test maintenance previously unidentified. "Prevalent Practices" at the Flight Research Center had begun to open the door for scheduling problems, personnel knowledge loss, and program management issues. Inspectors had been assigned to a research program, but, because of the unique characteristics and complex systems within the varying projects, they often lacked practical experience in areas they were responsible for. Theory and practice were imbalanced within projects and therefore knowledge gaps were evident. Investigators noticed that it had become common practice to reorganize or remove team members from projects without verifying a replacement

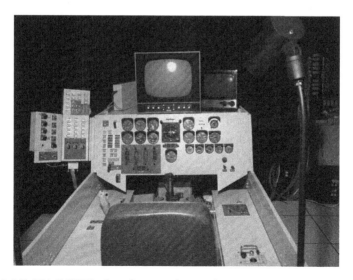

Figure 1.5 F-15A RPRV sub-scale ground control station at NASA Dryden Flight Research Center © NASA

member could be found with equal knowledge. Review committees had become ineffectual, and their findings nearly useless within the organization for establishing organizational consistency.

The F-15 Eagle RPRV program would go through a variety of changes and culminated with a change to the landing system entirely. After successfully landing after the MARS system had failed entirely, the Eagle was refitted with landing skids and the program adapted to land horizontally on the dried lake bed at Edward's Air Force Base. This model would go on to prove instrumental in establishing Spin Research and contributed directly to the safety of manned aircraft as well as unmanned.

In November, 1977—after a 2-year hiatus of the F-15 RPRV program— flights resumed under a new program called the Spin Research Vehicle (SRV) project (Merlin 1974). Research conducted was intended to evaluate the overall effect of the nose shape on spin susceptibility for modern high-performance jet engine fighter planes. This SRV program ended in 1981 after 72 flights with only two ground aborts, one aborted planned-captive flight, and 15 air aborts prior to launch. Of the 16 MARS recoveries, 13 had been successful with 5 landings occurring on the PIRA and 34 on the lake bed (Merlin 2001). The most important thing, for program management, was, "Did this thing do what they needed it to do?" and the resounding answer would come in how it fulfilled its mission role. In a 1974 journal article published with *Astronautics and Aeronautics*, R. Dale Reed wrote that, "If information obtained from this program avoids the loss of just one full-scale F-15, then the program will have been a tremendous bargain."

As a result of this F-15 RPRV program and the Spin Test results, the F-156 identified a dangerous "yaw-trip" problem found also within the full-scale F-15s equipped with an offset airspeed boom. This configuration had the potential to exhibit "abrupt departure characteristics in turning flight as angle of attack increased." As these results were being processed, both the F-15C and F-15 Strike Eagle were seen to have yaw-trip issues as they both had fuselage-hugging fuel tanks and offset nose-booms. With this research made available quickly, the problem was soon identified and alleviated fears that perhaps the F-15 might have an inherent flaw that would require extremely expensive redesign. The problem was quickly resolved and to this day, the F-15 RPRVs are seen as the savior to the F-15 manned fighter.

2 Technology adoption: A story of war and economics

If unmanned aircraft were not expected to grow into multi-billion dollar industries over the next few decades, there would be no need to examine the regulatory framework that governs this technology. Without a quickly approaching massive expansion in this market, the regulatory framework could be expected to handle the growth slowly and over time. The industry simply does not have that luxury as the expectations and needs for UAS expand exponentially and the need for quick investment and implementation continues. The estimated market growth for UAS is tremendous and every new release of estimation seems to swell that number. The year 2014 was to be the year of the drone, then it was 2015. Now, 2016 is expected to herald the coming of the robotic aerial revolution as drone racing pushes forward and new regulatory approaches are considered. All we really know for certain is that the potential impact of unmanned aircraft is tremendous. As one leader in the field puts it, "We're really at the beginning of our 20 year story. We won't understand the impact of drones for 20 years and likely not even then."

The state of UAS is in flux throughout the world as individual countries seek to promote differing restrictions—usually focusing on safety, privacy, or corporate concerns. Within the United States, the issue becomes more complicated as individual states have begun to pre-empt the federal government's role in regulating the airspace. Full integration in the national airspace will happen eventually, though some critics point out that it will require either more robust detect-and-avoid systems or a fundamental change in how we view airspace management. Concurrently to all of these efforts, individual state governments within the United States should not be able to usurp the power of governance solely given by Congress to the FAA. These states, and many municipalities, point to the Tenth Amendment of the Constitution that when Congress fails to legislate, the states have the innate right to do so. Unfortunately for the states, the FAA has acted under direction from congressional legislation, is intending to act through continued release of codified regulations, and has made clear that it is acting in a meaningful and appropriate manner.

The economic potential for UAS integration into the national airspace is extremely positive and, barring catastrophe, will continue to raise expectations as full integration moves forward. Time is a significant factor in these integration efforts as the international marketplace is growing exponentially; it is estimated that every day in which full integration is pushed back, "the United States loses $10 billion in potential economic impact . . ." translating to a loss of "$27.6 Million per day."

Competition between US domestic entities grows as well, as the six test center sites, who were expected to create "23,000 new jobs adding up to $12 Billion in wages, $720 Million in new tax revenues and an overall $23 Billion in total economic impact over 10 years . . ." to the states selected, have not panned out quite as well immediately as initially hoped. Languid regulatory confusion, easily accessed testing at military sites or government partner sites, and international ease of access has fostered dramatic competition between these test sites and their respective government representatives. These same test sites, if you ask leadership there, were not given the guidance, oversight, and freedom to pursue the types of operational approvals or certification and testing that would have been necessary in order to realize the ambitions of those who had initially applied for a test site.

The gains from full integration moving forward are very high, especially in the current US economy seeking high-paying, highly skilled manufacturing jobs. As a result, it is clear that a political element exists in moving forward for the UAS integration effort at the municipal, state, and federal levels. Only in the last couple of years have we seen the creation of new lobbying groups and "educational" groups rising to power in the industry. Where before the Association for Unmanned Vehicle Systems International (AUVSI) represented their 7,500-member organizations to the government and pushed forward their political agenda, new representative groups have found voices, and funding, by sUAS companies, operators and manufacturers such as the Small UAV Coalition, a plethora of Washington and Silicon Valley-based lobbying groups such as Denton's LLP or AUVSA, opposition groups such as AOPA, ALPA, IFALPA, and industry representative groups for farmers, miners, and more. All of these groups are playing a huge role in developing regulations and it is having the usual "sausage grinder" effect on policy.

The full economic impact of integration of UAS is estimated to be "$13.6 Billion in the first three years of integration and grow[ing] sustainably . . . cumulating in more than $82.1 Billion between 2015 and 2025" (Jenkins and Vasigh 2013). By accounting for standard technology adoption rate models and using the Japanese adoption rate of UAS for their markets as the input, it is estimated that integration will create "70,000 new jobs, of which 34,000 are manufacturing, within the first three years of adoption." By 2025 this job creation is expected to account for 103,776 new jobs nationwide and provide $482 million in tax revenues for those 11 years (Jenkins and Vasigh 2013).

While the expectations of the industry are growing with every new application that is discovered or any new technological enabler, the assumptions in the cited study are flawed, but acts as one of the only studies available to show the true economic impact of integration of sUAS. These assumptions include an unrealistic belief in the adoption of agricultural UAS throughout the United States and the globe. The agricultural demands of the United States are very different from those in Japan because of much larger farm sizes. Farms in Japan average four hectares while the United States average farm size is 400 hectares. Japanese farms are also more vertical in nature while in the United States are much flatter. Further, the economic conditions in Japan that require a focus on automation and technology developments to make up for an aging workforce do not necessarily exist in the United States market, and cannot be directly applied throughout the world. Europe will have very different adoption due to cultural and market forces that differ from Asia, as well South America and Australia. Though flawed, the basic conclusion—that UAS economies are set to grow expeditiously upon full integration—is completely accurate, in markets where we have an analogous experience. Rather than chemical dispersion UAS, agricultural applications have already seen tremendous use of Geographical Information Systems (GIS) and photogrammetric modeling based upon imagery captured by small quadcopters or fixed-wing aircraft. LiDAR (Light Detection And Ranging) is proving to be a very successful tool across industries, and soon delivery drones will pock the sky above.

The use and production of drones increases daily throughout the world, and it is supposed that the United States and the UK likewise lose leadership in the industry as strict regulations hold back innovation. As recently as 15 years ago, the United States and Israel were the sole exporters of military and commercial UAS (Jenkins and Vasigh 2013). Now, China, Russia, Iran, Australia, Brazil, Germany, Turkey, and Canada have finalized their development programs of UAVs and have begun exporting the systems internationally.

Figure 2.1 Drone inspections lead the way in commercial application for UAS. Image compilation by Harrison Wolf

General Atomics' Predator™, Boeing's ScanEagle™ and Firescout™, and Northrop Grumman's Global Hawk™ are no longer the only systems for purchase internationally as Turkey's Anka™, Europe's nEUROn™, Australia's Camcopter-S™, and South Africa's Seeker 400™ offer similar capabilities at lower regional costs (Governor's Office of the Commonwealth of Virginia 2014). The competitive marketplace continues to grow as all countries seek to develop new technical, high-paying manufacturing and design positions in both military and commercial environments—both necessitating regulatory frameworks that are open, safe, and secure.

Larger UAS systems, as described above, do not seem to be the largest growing markets for unmanned aircraft and yet they are still vastly important to the military. Northrop Grumman recently announced their full focus on the tail-sitting strike drone launched from ships and their continued sales and support of the Global Hawk (Norris and DiMascio 2015). The US Navy Secretary Ray Mabus even announced that the F-35 "should be, and almost certainly, will be the last manned strike fighter aircraft the Department of the Navy will ever buy or fly." While the Air Force continues demands for manned fighters, many in the industry see all military aircraft heading toward unmanned or optionally piloted variants.

Commercial applications for unmanned systems are endless and offer environmentally and economically friendly alternatives to manned aviation without necessitating huge investments in infrastructure, or altering the "day-to-day" business operations at airports on the ground or in the air. Wildfire mapping has become a constant mission profile that drones have been lauded for at all levels of government—the firefighters that use them call them "life-savers," "mission critical," and often "their best friends in the air." As drones are able to take away the need for pilots to risk their lives over smoke-laden flames to identify hot spots, direction changes, wind alterations, or dwindling areas that need less attention, risk is reduced significantly, increases on-site performance, and enables new high-risk operations never dreamed of before. Farmers throughout the nation are utilizing personally owned and operated fixed-wing aircraft such as the Penguin-B™ or SenseFly™ for "remote sensing" and "precision application," to scan plants for health problems, locate disease outbreaks, record growth and hydration rates, and develop more effective and efficient spray techniques to better cover fields and plants thereby reducing pesticide and herbicide run-off, reducing operating costs in the air, on the ground, and to the environment. The agricultural industries have found great benefit from unmanned systems use. UAS companies have grown quickly, offering different services with differing technologies. New sensor payloads are being developed to industry-specific needs. An example of this is seen in the attention that technology companies are paying specifically to agricultural needs. If you were interested you could look at private investment in these companies, or look to operational approvals by the FAA to show its growth. If you had an investor's pitch in Silicon Valley you might think of showing your addressable markets and segmentation, showing 3x growth year over year in all major indicators. However, to me, the best way to illustrate the health and potential opportunities of a new market is to show all of the recently developed capabilities for this segment, and the need for refinement, application, and their widespread adoption.

To date operations within agriculture have mainly consisted of:

- Terrain, rock, tree, and obstacle mapping
- Hybrid lifecycle charting
- Chlorophyll damage detection
- Ground-covering profiling
- Wind profile and wind-shear assessment
- Temperature and barometric pressure profiling
- Spore, dust, and pollen counts
- Water quality assessment and survey
- Methane, ammonia, and CO_2 sensing
- Trait assessment for breeding
- Wireless data collection from ground sensors
- Plant status tracking
- Crop status (growing stage, yield estimates, etc.)
- Precision agriculture prescription data
- Tiling/drainage evaluation and survey
- Time-saving pre-assessment for field tasks
- Oblique shots for vegetative growth analysis
- Drainage estimates and topography
- Planting evaluation and replanting requirements
- Pathogen introduction and tracking.

Farmers and firefighters are not the only professionals enjoying the benefits of drone-supplemented missions. Those individuals who are responsible for disaster management and crisis first response, thermal infrared power-line surveys, oil and gas exploration, telecommunications, weather monitoring, aerial imaging/mapping, television news coverage, sporting events and moviemaking, and environmental monitoring will all be able to incorporate drones for cost-saving, but not necessarily mission profile changing methods. What unmanned aircraft allow the user to do is not reinvent how information is gathered but simply make it easier, more cost-effective, and more efficient to gather that information. Farmers can plant crops with less pesticide and herbicide for greater crop yields and better timed planting; maximizing growth times in ground and sugar production and turnover. Firemen can fight fire with up-to-the minute knowledge of how the fire is acting beyond the front lines in a safer, more secure environment. Oil and gas producers can monitor their flare stacks and pipelines with less usage of manned aircraft reducing the strain on infrastructure and reducing their use of fossil fuels. These uses all amount to productive gains with direct social and economic benefit not calculated in the economic impact report as they are indirect, but clear, benefits of integrating unmanned aircraft systems into the national airspace.

Public safety is the second largest economic application for the UAS industry with law enforcement officers and agencies eager to use drones. This is the stimulus for many state legislatures' limitation on the use of drones, and Virginia's complete ban of law enforcement use in 2013 due to an odd coupling of both Tea Party and ACLU political up-swell based on privacy concerns. The opportunity for drones to make a positive impact on public safety is extreme. Law enforcement agencies at all levels are urging the FAA, local municipalities, and state government to develop clear and concise regulation that will help them define when and where they can use drones for surveillance, reconnaissance, search warrant execution, missing person searches, operational security, perimeter maintenance, and other missions that will still ensure privacy is protected for those in an area in which drones are operating (Subbaraman 2013). Fixed-wing aircraft and quad or hex-copter are in high demand for operations with armed suspects, where turning the wrong corner will get an officer or suspect injured or killed senselessly. Preventing law enforcement officers from using drones results in needless injuries and damage to property; this could be easily prevented by incorporating unmanned aircraft systems. The opportunity to develop thriving economic industries throughout the world is here and it is now; it is up to the state, local, and national legislatures to embrace the future and all the wealth it brings, or fall by the wayside in the new, competitive, marketplace.

Beyond these very practical and proven approaches to unmanned system flight are the innovators and entrepreneurs who are not transforming a current manned flight to unmanned flight, but providing new approaches to old problems. Videography, cinematography, surveying, and real estate are all applications for small unmanned aircraft platforms at prices that define them as "consumer." These platforms verge on being called toys and are manufactured by DJI™, 3DR™, Parrot™, and any number of other startups. The list of promising startups in the hardware grows all of the time, and by the time they are listed there is a good chance the list has changed. What we can do is to list locations to look for these up-and-comers and that will be covered in a later section.

The use of drones internationally is skyrocketing and is estimated to surpass manned aviation—especially in agricultural farming—within the next decade; the "consensus being that the agricultural market will be at least ten times the public safety market" (Deloitte 2012). Already farmers throughout the world have adapted to using medium-sized, helicopter-based platforms to maintain and grow their lands. Demand for these platforms is increasing and it is becoming clear that unmanned aviation is a vital element in the future of all flight. While farmers in Japan now spray roughly 30 per cent of their farms with pesticide from unmanned helicopters, park rangers in South Africa patrol their 3,000-acre wildlife reserves for signs of rhino and elephant poachers. As American Customs and Border Protection agents seek drug smugglers, illegal border crossings, and gun-runners along the Southwest American borders, so too do Canadian mining companies use similar systems to survey forests for oil, mineral, and gas deposits in the extreme north. The opportunities are endless, and the international markets are adapting to motivate, support, develop, and apply these new technologies quickly. The only question is, how will American companies and governments react?

Case study: The Yamaha RMAX

History of the Yamaha RMAX

The Yamaha RMAX™ Type II G & Type II are Yamaha's agricultural unmanned aircraft solutions to farming. In 1983, Yamaha Motor Company began developing an unmanned helicopter for crop dusting as the result of a request from the Ministry of Agriculture, Forestry and Fishery of Japan (Yamaha Motor Australia 2013). Initial research led to the development and completion of the first agricultural unmanned aircraft vehicle (UAV), the "R-50," industrial-use unmanned helicopter in 1987. The payload of 20kg was considered the first practical-use unmanned helicopter for crop dusting as other vehicles' payload limitations offered little utility compared to more traditional farming.

As the early 1990s heralded a re-focusing on robotic technology and the Japanese economies recovered from the late 1970s and early 1980s stagflation, the Ministry of Agriculture officially announced a policy of promotion for the use of unmanned helicopters in crop dusting for rice farming (1991). The use of unmanned helicopters in rice farms had significant promise as the average age of the Japanese rice farmer increased and heirs to these farmers chose other, more urban, professions. A strengthening of restrictions on pest-control crop dusting by airplanes due to increasing diversity and the spread of residential areas into agricultural areas, demanded a more precise and less environmentally impactful delivery of pest-control.

In the late 1990s competition began to emerge to Yamaha's successful industrial UAS. As competition grew, a development in control mechanisms and stabilization contributed to the creation of the YACS (Yamaha Attitude Control System) in March 1995. This YACS made learning the control of the helicopter much easier and reduced the major hindrance to widespread adoption; until then the helicopter had been considered very difficult to fly. As a result, it became "possible for most people to become proficient at crop dusting just after a short period of training . . . this made the benefits accessible to many more users." In October 1997, the RMAX industrial-use unmanned helicopter was released featuring greater payload capacity and greater ease of operation.

The demand for RMAX industrial-use helicopters exploded and much of the metrics published showing the adoption rates of UAS in the United States is modeled on the adoption rates of the RMAX industrial-use helicopter from 2000 to today (Jenkins and Vasigh 2013). According to Yamaha, there are roughly 2,400 RMAX helicopters flying in Japan, representing 77 per cent market share in industrial unmanned aircraft. Meanwhile the number of qualified pilots is roughly 7,500 nationwide. In 2001, there were 310,000 hectares serviced by RMAX helicopters.

Yamaha is currently looking into industrial uses other than agriculture. With the advent and widespread adoption of GPS control, the refinement of autonomous flight systems, and the need for unmanned operations, Yamaha is hoping to lead the world in successful unmanned helicopter operations for industrial use.

Specifications and features

The Yamaha RMAX has the below specifications and features. All information is taken directly from the Yamaha Product Specification & Features pages and represents the manufacturer's selling points as facts (Yamaha Motor Australia 2013). Among these features illustrated by Yamaha as the most significant sales points for consumers are the YACS warning light/GPS indicator light, self-monitoring function, moving wheels/handling grips, main rotor characteristics, dispersal ranges, multiple helicopter control mechanisms, and flight characteristics. A short description is below:

YACS—A warning light that alerts the operator to any potential problems whilst in flight. These lights are easy to see, and make it possible to confirm at a glance that all systems are working properly.

Self-monitor function—The self-monitor function enables a helicopter to make a self-check on each part of the helicopter before flying and notifies the operator of defects.

Moving wheels / Handling grips—Wheels on the landing gear enable the RMAX to be moved by a single operator. With a total weight of 100kg, the RMAX can be loaded by two people.

Main rotor—The main rotor will come to a stop within approximately 20 seconds with the rotor brake used after the engine is stopped. Being able to quickly stop the rotors increases safety and allows for fast refilling.

Flight characteristics—High-performance GPS increases helicopter stability, speed, altitude and directional control making on-target dispersal simple, safe, and accurate. Ease of hovering, braking and speed control, and constant speed allow for better control and maintenance of stability in a variety of maneuvers.

Specifications

Performance

Load capacity	28kg
Practical range	(Visual range) up to 400m
Control system	YACS-G (RMAX Type II G) / YMCS (RMAX Type II)

Dimensions

Main rotor diameter	3,130mm
Trail rotor diameter	535mm
Overall length	2,750mm / 3,630mm (with rotor)
Overall width	720mm
Overall height	1,080mm

Engine

Type	2-cycle, horizontally opposed 2-cylinder
Cylinder displacement	246cc
Maximum output	15.4kw
Starting system	Electric starter
Fuel	Regular gasoline mixed with 2-cycle engine oil

Liquid sprayer

Cassette tank capacity	8 liters × 2 tanks
Discharge method	Double-acting piston with flat nozzle
Discharge rate	1.3–2.0/minute (speed-linking method)
Nozzle pitch	1340mm
Sprayer weight	7.4kg

Granular sprayer

Hopper capacity	13 liters × 2 tanks
Discharge method	Impeller (300mm dia.)
Discharge rate	2.5kg/minute (when spraying 1kg/10a)
Impeller rotational speed	800rmp
Sprayer weight	7.0kg

Case analysis: Korean accident investigation 2009

Narrative

At 8:10, on August 3, 2009, a 46-year-old pilot of a Korean aerial spray company and the aerial spray team leader, aged 56, arrived at the Osu Agricultural Cooperative (Osu AC) building to prepare for an aerial spray mission utilizing the unmanned aircraft, Yamaha RMAX #S7044. Another pilot who was supposed to fly this mission had taken vacation leave and therefore the executive director, normally in charge of guidance and economy, aged 51 and already at work from early in the morning, volunteered to join the aerial spray team to act as the co-pilot.

The team of three departed the Osu AC around 9:00 and arrived at the morning work site around 9:40. The team carried out aerial spray work on the paddies of about 4 hectares from 10:40 to 12:10. After finishing their morning assignment, they planned an afternoon mission of aerial spray work on another section of the owner's paddy which was located close to the morning aerial spray site. They departed for a long lunch to return later and finish their work.

Figure 2.2 Map of the flight environment for Yamaha RMAX

After having lunch at a nearby restaurant, the aerial spray team and the paddy owner arrived at the location for the next mission shown.

According to statements of witnesses taken later, the aerial spray team made preparations for the coming mission. This included "identification of obstacles in the area scheduled for the afternoon aerial spray," dilution of agricultural pesticides, a work briefing, and a visual check of #S7044.

The aerial spray mission was planned to be conducted by flying to the left and right from southwest to northeast illustrated in the picture below.

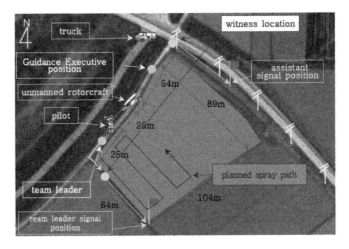

Figure 2.3 Timeline of the Yamaha RMAX accident flight

The pilot started the engine while the other aerial spray team members moved away about 15 meters from #S7044. The pilot increased the engine RPM to a lift speed. Once confirming that the #S7044 took off, the aerial spray team leader as well as the guidance executive who had replaced the other pilot as co-pilot for this mission, started to move to the locations they had been designated in order to offer signals for boundary identification for the pilot.

While moving to the assistant signal position, the guidance executive "turned around two times to watch the pilot and the flying of #S7044." The guidance executive stated later to investigators that when he turned around for the second time to watch the pilot, he saw the helicopter approaching fast with its tail toward the pilot and the pilot falling down after making a few backward steps.

The aerial spray team leader also stated that he turned around to watch the pilot while he was moving to his position; however, he did not see the moment of impact and only saw the pilot had fallen down following the accident.

The pilot died immediately after collision with the unmanned aircraft on a farm road about 18m away from the take-off location.

Pilot background

The head pilot and sole fatality of this accident was hired by Osu Agricultural Collaborative in May 2003, and had been working at a local rice processing center (RPC). Osu AC had decided in 2003 to employ an unmanned rotorcraft for aerial spray as a part of a farming support project for AC members, and he was selected to become the pilot with one other pilot for training.

The pilot completed the initial training course provided by Yamaha, February 11–29, 2009, in accordance with a project plan of the Osu AC and obtained a skill certification in July 2008 from the Korean Agricultural Unmanned Helicopter Association.[3] This pilot had routinely worked at the RPC during normal work hours, and in the summer months acted as a pilot for aerial spray.

The pilot's total flight time could not be identified since he did not maintain a flight log.

Operation of radio control box

Frequency: 72Mhz
Coverage (effective / maximum): 150–200m / 600m

The UA ascends or descends when the throttle control stick on the left front of the radio control box is moved up or down. When the throttle is moved left or right, the head changes respective to the movement. If the control stick on the right front is moved to the left or right, the aircraft banks right. When the control stick is pulled down, the swashplate of the unmanned rotorcraft activates so that the rotorcraft moves rearward and vice versa. The Figure 2.4 shows this movement.

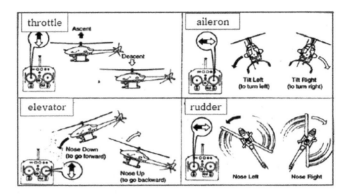

Figure 2.4 Flight dynamics and corresponding controls for Yamaha RMAX

Figure 2.5 Yamaha RMAX remote controller prior to accident

The radio control box also comes equipped with throttle, rudder, pitch, and aileron switches for ease of use of the pilot. These are shown in Figure 2.5.

Damage

Main rotor

The main rotor is made of a composite material and a balancing stick of metal. The middle portion of main rotor blades was broken by ground impact as shown in Figure 2.6.

Skid

The skid of the unmanned helicopter was bent and damaged by ground impact.

Figure 2.6 Post-crash image of Yamaha RMAX full body

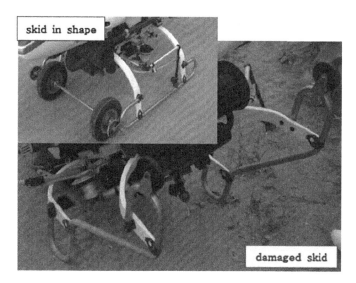

Figure 2.7 Post-crash image of Yamaha RMAX skids

Tail boom

The tail boom was broken at the joint with the forward fuselage and the aft fuselage.

Radio control box (ground control station)

Both the front and rear case of the radio control box were destroyed and the inside circuit board had been partially damaged due to collision with rotor blades.

Figure 2.8 Post–crash image of Yamaha RMAX tail section

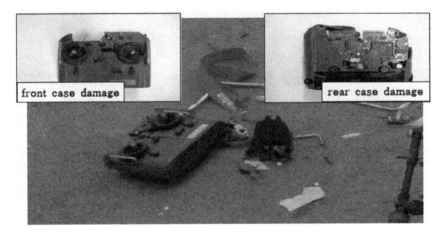

Figure 2.9 Post–crash image of the remote controller used during RMAX flight

Safety and history of maintenance

The #S7044 unmanned rotorcraft was maintained in accordance with the manufacturer's manual specification and was certified for its safety on May 2009 by the Korean Transportation Safety Authority. No defect was recorded in the pre-flight or post-flight check items of the 2009 flight check log maintained by the Osu AC pilots.

According to witnesses, the #S7044 had no signs of abnormal condition to the airframe or abnormal response from the radio control box that morning.

The #S7044 had previously been in one accident. This accident occurred when the pilot—the same pilot as the 2009 accident—flew into an electrical wire and crashed during its inaugural aerial spray flight. The rotorcraft was repaired on August 17, 2008—the day of the accident—by Moosung Aviation and returned to normal operation.

Other facts

The take-off area for this accident is located roughly 5km south of a corporate office, and is on a paved farm road with an average width of 3.3m, lying parallel to the embankment road south of the Dundeok Bridge as shown in Figure 2.10.

* Weather conditions for the day of the accident were:
  14:00—Wind: Easterly wind 1.7m/s
  Temp: 23.6 Degrees C
  Humidity: 74 per cent
  15:00—Wind: Southwesterly wind 1.2m/s
  Temp: 24.1 Degrees C
  Humidity: 72 per cent
* Communication was not considered a factor in this accident.
* Precision analysis of the onboard flight data recorder found no indication of malfunction on board the #S7044.

Figure 2.10 Crash site of Yamaha RMAX

Training

The initial training course conducted by Moosung Aviation is intended to provide the pilots with on-site training focusing on safety prior to each aerial spray season. However, according to the Moosung Aviation personnel, "the interest and participation rate of the managers and pilots were not so high." The on-site training of 2009 covered a variety of topics including pre-flight checklists, maintenance examinations, proper positioning of switches, and proper maneuvers for the unmanned rotorcraft.

Certification of pilot qualifications

Pilots of unmanned rotorcraft are not required to obtain any certificate from the Minister of Land, Transport, and Maritime Affairs.[4] Therefore, the Korean Agricultural Unmanned Helicopter Association—an incorporated association— issues pilot's skill certificates to association members such as Osu AC. Evaluation for issuing the skill certificates is charged to the training instructors of the importer (Moosung Aviation). The average pass rate for these trainings and evaluations has historically been 96 per cent and above, with a 100 per cent pass rate recorded in 2008.

No close reading of the operator manual was required by the training course, but certain portions of the manual were highlighted. The operator's manual was written and published by Yamaha Motors, Inc. and distributed by Moosung Aviation. The manual contains safety notes, specifications, pre-flight preparations and checks, and flight procedures.

Specific notes relating to this accident were highlighted by accident investigators:

1. At least three trained persons are necessary for aerial spraying.
2. Since operation of an unmanned rotorcraft brings about mental fatigue, flight for more than one hour without rest should be avoided.
3. A person with an unhealthy condition is not allowed to fly the unmanned rotorcraft.
4. Staying within 15m around unmanned rotorcraft is not allowed until main rotor blades completely stop.
5. Flight is not allowed when windspeeds, measured at 1.5m above ground level, are more than 3m/s.

Pre-flight preparations and checks mentioned by investigators:

1. Before flight, battery charge, operation of the radio control box and the antenna should be checked.
2. Operation check of the radio control box is to verify the operational condition of the alarm and output lamp of the radio control box.

Checklist items did not address or instruct the direct checking of switch, button, or toggle positions.

A revolutionary technology on an evolutionary path:
An interview with Michael Toscano

Technology commercialization, the transfer of theoretical or immature technology to commercial markets from research and development for public use (military/law enforcement), is one of the most important elements of the UAS story. To help shed light on this topic, Michael Toscano agreed to discuss his understanding and insights to the unmanned systems industry. His involvement in the unmanned industry began 20 years before his connection with the industry-leading organization AUVSI, of which he acted as President and CEO from 2008 to 2013. Prior to holding the position of President and CEO of AUVSI, Michael was a Program Manager for Research and Development for Nuclear Security in the Office of the Deputy Assistant to the Secretary of Defense for Nuclear Matters, and Chairman of the Physical Security Equipment Action Group (PSEAG). He has seen his fair share of unmanned robotic systems develop, mature, commercialize, and be replaced by newer technology. In the beginning, he says, his experience focused on predominantly ground robotics, but as robotics in general began to mature, the military and government began seeing similar problems shared among the ground, air, sea, and space sectors; it all came down to safety. Toscano's viewpoint is one of tempered optimism, because, as he puts it, "it's 50:50" whether or not unmanned systems will be the savior of mankind, or its destroyer. It will be one of the two, and we're not sure which it will be. Michael continues his career even through retirement, sitting as a chairperson of the Senior Advisory Group for the FAA's Center of Excellence, providing strategic advisement and analysis for state and local governments, and simply as a mentor for those looking to achieve great things in this rapidly evolving field.

When you hear him speak, Michael Toscano comes off clearly as an avid student of both history and technology. His explanations and examples for where the UAS industry is heading, and how the public interface of that technology will impact its future, provide great context for the overall discussion of technology development. "For any unmanned systems," Michael begins, "the most paramount thing to understand is that it is all about safety. For any new technology, the question must be raised, what is the risk acceptance?" This point is not lost on the reader of this book; however, he means it in a way perhaps left unaddressed. In this context, risk acceptance is examining the benefits and detriments of any technology, to determine if the negatives of the technology can be tolerated for the benefits. "Risk acceptance is on a sliding scale." Toscano elaborates:

> Look at the automobile. We're going to kill 38,000 people this year alone in the United States. I can say that because we did that last year. We're

going to have about 6.5 million accidents that will cost us about $330 billion in medical costs and damages, and yet we drive cars every day.

The point is a significant one. Our safety tolerance for cars is far lower than any other mode of transportation. We acknowledge that the risk of driving a car is high, and yet we still allow cars to exist and that technology to be used because the benefits of movement, at-will transportation, outweigh the potential injury in our own risk assessment. At the moment, the UAS industry has not clearly defined the benefits of UAS to such an acceptable range and it is unclear if that will be the case.

So the question is, what will change the public's acceptance of risk and understanding to allow UAS to flourish? Toscano's answer is that a number of factors can come together to foster positive change and continue to drive the industry forward. What this industry needs is what some companies are already doing:

> When Jeff Bezos went on 60 minutes and said we will do this in the future, and Amazon says we're going to do it, and then Google steps up and says we too are going to do it, that is leadership taking the next step. They are saying that we understand how emotionally difficult this will be, but that this is a better mouse trap and we know it's a better way to get things delivered so we will gravitate towards it.

Ultimately, Michael believes, it will be a combination of leadership and technology maturation that will drive this industry forward positively. The positives have already been illustrated well enough to commercial early adopters and that, simply put, "The genie can't be put back in the bottle."

So, what of hindrances that can set back the industry, or already do? Mr. Toscano believes that the privacy issue has been so misleading to the public, and so politicized, that real damage is being done to the efforts of the UMS industry unfairly. "The privacy issue" Toscano warns:

> is the latest way that those afraid of natural change exert their discomfort. With all the sensors in the world today, anytime you step out in public you're able to be observed. What you really care about is your data . . . and that is much more a cyber security issue than a hardware issue like unmanned systems.

Perhaps the most enlightening approach to UMS is how we view the past as it applies to the future, and Michael Toscano provides lucid and applicable examples of how the past is paralleling the future. When people decry the loss of jobs, Michael points to the very nature of disruptive technologies to both reduce and create jobs. "Look at the phone booth." He begins:

> You used to have all of these phones on every corner with boxes of money that would have to be collected. Those were jobs. People went around

to each phone booth and collected money. With the advent of the cellphone, and other mobile technologies, the phone booth became obsolete. Those jobs vanished. Some would see that as a negative, however among the benefits of this new technology were new, higher paying jobs.

The cellphone also offers other examples that Michael touched on to reflect the state of the unmanned aircraft industry today:

> Not too long ago, cellphones were a cumbersome, heavy, nearly bread loaf size technology that dropped calls half of the time. Consumers demanded more and the technology didn't see wide adoption until it was more refined. The same is what we're seeing with unmanned aircraft. The systems of today pale in comparison to the technology we will see 30 years from now. Just like the internet, unmanned systems is a revolutionary technology on an evolutionary path. It's disrupting more industries than we see. So, don't look at where the technology is today, but look at where it is in the maturation process . . . When you look at unmanned systems, the first thing to understand is that it is a capability that improves how to do things today. It will eliminate some jobs, it will create more jobs, and it will change laws.

Unmanned aircraft are not alone in their disruptive nature, and Michael Toscano discusses unmanned systems in a context that includes land, sea, air, and space unmanned robotics. While this book is focused on the aerial side of unmanned systems, his point of view that the same problem exists across all modalities is a fascinating one. Toscano points out that:

> If you look at today, it is easier to fly a Boeing 787 from Los Angeles through automation than it is to pick a strawberry or take keys out of your pocket . . . we'll see the same technology developments from unmanned systems continue to cross over into manned aviation

and perhaps even further. To see how robotics across modalities are related and evolving, you only have to look at the rapid changes since Michael's time with the Department of Defense. During his tenure leading the robotics program office, Toscano points out that the fastest we could process information had a half-millisecond delay, but at 40-50 miles per hour you've killed someone if you're talking ground robotics. Now, Google and others are building cars that can respond in a real-time manner and it will just get better with time.

These technologies are moving across industries. If we look to cellphones, the "apps" industry that evolved in an ecosystem of entertainment and productivity is now prevalent in wearables, home software and hardware, and in the automobile. Cars are becoming Internet hotspots while a blender can be controlled by a smartwatch.

When asked what is the fundamental and the most important enabling technology to the UMS field, he responded:

> The holy grail for enabling technologies is detect and avoid. We can replicate the sonar of a dolphin and the olfactory of a dog. Someday we will replicate how birds fly in the sky and fish swim in the sea without running into each other. Once we can do that, we will have minimal accidents, which means, we don't need protection, we don't need armor. Cars would be 50% lighter. We don't need the structure or airbags. Because of this, the materials are reduced and accidents are diminished. Eliminate the accidents, or 90% of them, and we have changed the whole equation—that's what this technology can do.

I guess the last thing to say about why Michael Toscano is so adamant about the future of unmanned systems is that, from an engineer's point of view, it just makes sense, and I tend to agree. When it comes down to why our transportation systems will all go unmanned, he says:

> Depending on which transportation report you read, some say 87—93% of all accidents are caused by a human being. As an engineer, if you see 90% of failures caused by one thing, that's the thing you fix. Eliminate the accidents, or 90% of them, and you have changed the whole equation. That's why we'll have driverless cars and that's why we'll see unmanned aircraft. Just like the internet, unmanned aircraft systems is a revolutionary technology on an evolutionary path.

Truly, unmanned systems and robotics are changing the way even the concept of ownership is seen. While the sharing economy has continued to develop through companies like Uber, Lyft, and AirBnB, demographic shifts have shown younger generations less interested in owning their first car and more interested in developing technologies. It is not uncommon for a 16-year-old to ask for coding lessons, a new computer rig, or digital currency for a videogame rather than owning a car (Rosenthal 2013). As driverless vehicles grow in availability and use, it's clear that private ownership will likely be replaced by sharing services or some other method that even today is unknown or unclear. We are seeing a revolutionary technology that is evolving rapidly. Every iteration is something to behold, and because of visionary leaders such as Michael Toscano, who recognized that his tenure as AUVSI would see the true introduction of unmanned aircraft to commercial markets and made it his goal to help that process along, we can be sure that the unmanned systems industry will continue to grow, change, and adapt in ways unknown.

3 International standards and regulations

The leading manufacturer of commercial and hobbyist unmanned aircraft, SZ DJI Inc.™, is from China (Nicas and Murphy 2014). The most notable High Altitude Long Endurance (HALE) operations of military unmanned systems, General Atomics, Predator MQ-9™, are flown in Afghanistan, but controlled much of the time in American bases at home. Tactical and manportable systems are capable of being launched pneumatically, as with the Insitu Scan Eagle™, or by hand, like the AeroVironment Puma™ and Ravens™ often over borders and international boundaries. Whereas in the past, pilots were responsible for the aircraft they were piloting and could be easily made responsible for any actions in which a state found grievance or need for action, UAS offer a unique and new challenge to international regulations and standards. The assumption of easily determining a pilot in command (PIC) for a particular flight has changed as operations have changed. A number of entities are working together to bring the formation and harmonization of international standards to this rapidly evolving industry, but the task is not easily accomplished.

The International Civil Aviation Organization (ICAO) is the entity responsible for harmonizing aviation operations and certification between its member states with "the safe and efficient development of civil aviation." Established on December 7, 1944, ICAO brought together 52 nations—known now as the original member states. These 52 nations came together under the auspices of creating an international system for ensuring the safe operation of aircraft. They met for a Convention on Civil Aviation, later renamed and now known as the Chicago Convention. On April 4, 1947, ICAO became a specialized agency of the United Nations linked to the Economic and Social Council (ECOSOC). This non-governmental organization (NGO) is now responsible for developing standards or recommended practices for aviation and is recognized the world over as the leader in aviation safety.

It is vital for students of unmanned aircraft, aviation, or simply transportation to know and understand the approach to international standards heralded by ICAO. This international organization offers a model for working together to create a safer, more unified, and better approach to global relationships, technological adaptation, and leadership agnostic to national interests.

Figure 3.1 Man flying UAV helicopter with video camera © John Wollwerth

ICAO's guidance can come in essentially two forms—a Standard or a Recommend Practice. The differences between these two types of recommendation are very important as they are also reflected throughout the regulatory and legislative environments of the United States and every member nation that is a signatory to the Chicago Convention. A Standard is defined by ICAO as, "any specification for physical characteristics, configuration, material, performance, personnel, or procedures, the uniform application of which is recognized as necessary for the safety or regularity of international air navigation and to which member states will conform." These standards are therefore to be considered requirements for its member states to enforce in their own aviation programs. An example of this could be minimum length of runways, how or when a country's language may be used for communication, or what materials can be used in the development of a commercial aircraft. Standards cannot be taken lightly; every member state has agreed to these standards as they are recognized as requisite to maintaining their good standing with ICAO.

A Recommend Practice is any specification that is recognized as being "desirable in the interest of safety, regularity, or efficiency of international air navigation and to which member states will endeavor to conform." The difference may seem very small to the untrained eye, however the distinction between a "must comply" and a "may comply" is vital to accomplishing integration of new aircraft, new systems, or the indoctrination of innovative business practice. As many say, bureaucracies can be tough to alter, and even tougher to change quickly. Imagine trying to force sovereign governments to agree to changes for one of the most important transportation systems in the world. As you can imagine, it is very difficult and requires extensive political capital. While most nations understand the importance of complying with non-governmental recommendations in the interest of safety, there can be push-back on the adoption of standard or recommended practices.

The role of debating, updating, changing, and publishing these standards and recommended practices falls to ICAO's Air Navigation Commission (AN). The AN plans, coordinates, and examines all of ICAO's activities in the field of air navigation and is populated by 15 members who have been appointed by the council from among nominated member states. Any changes are voted upon by this council and if approved will be released to member states. Upon completion of this approval process, standards become binding on all member nations of ICAO while recommendations remain non-binding though any member nation that finds standards impractical can file a difference under Article 38 of the Chicago Convention.

All standards and recommended practices (SARPS) that have been published by ICAO are included and divided into 19 Annexes to the Chicago Convention. The easiest way to think about this is to understand that ICAO is essentially a civil aviation authority—such as the United States' FAA or the UK CAA for the United Kingdom—for the world and each nation state acts as the aviation operator for their country. ICAO's publications are pointed toward aviation organizations that have control over access to airspace, and therefore their best practices are intended for an audience of regulators, authorities, military, and other government agencies. While the audience is often state programs, operators to the public and manufacturers must still know these SARPs as they will need to comply with them down the road. These Annexes are divided into the following categories and subjects noted in Table 3.1.

While ICAO's role has changed over time, its fundamental work relates to ensuring that member nations all over the globe establish and follow best practices for aviation safety and security. In order to help promote the best practices, and to cultivate greater international harmonization, ICAO often takes a leadership role in promoting research that increases safety and helps to neutralize risks to the aviation industry. ICAO, therefore, is seen as a very important stakeholder in the unmanned aircraft story and perhaps one of the most important when looking to the future of unmanned aircraft regulations internationally. It is ICAO's advanced awareness that heralds the unmanned systems integration of Safety Management Systems (SMS) among other very important best practices. Most importantly, ICAO has now begun integrating UAS into the Annex system and, when applicable, addresses these various Annexes to UAS technologies.

While ICAO publishes final standards and recommendations for aviation within these annexes, and indeed there have been inclusions of UAS in Annex 6, 9, and 19, the most important publications that ICAO has put out referencing unmanned aircraft comes from ICAO Document 10019 An/507, *Manual on*

Table 3.1 ICAO list of annexes

Annex 1	Personnel Licensing—licensing of flight crews, air traffic controllers, and aircraft maintenance personnel
Annex 2	Rules of the Air—rules relating to the conduct of visual and instrument flights
Annex 3	Meteorological Services—provision of meteorological services for international air navigation and reporting of meteorological observations from aircraft
Annex 4	Aeronautical Charts—specifications for aeronautical charts for use in international aviation
Annex 5	Units of Measurement—dimensional systems to be used in air-ground communications
Annex 6	Operation of Aircraft. Part I: International Commercial Air Transport; Part II: International General Aviation; Part III: International Operations–Helicopters. These specifications will ensure in similar operations throughout the world a level of safety above a prescribed minimum
Annex 7	Aircraft Nationality and Registration Marks—requirements for registration and identification of aircraft
Annex 8	Airworthiness of Aircraft—certification and inspection of aircraft according to uniform procedures
Annex 9	Facilitation—simplification of customs, immigration, and health inspection regulations at international airports
Annex 10	Aeronautical Telecommunications—standardization of communications equipment and systems and of communications procedures
Annex 11	Air Traffic Services—establishment and operation of air traffic control, flight information, and alerting services
Annex 12	Search and Rescue—organization and operation of facilities and services necessary for search and rescue
Annex 13	Aircraft Accident Investigation—uniformity in the notification, investigation, and reporting of aircraft accidents
Annex 14	Aerodromes—specifications for the design and equipment of aerodromes
Annex 15	Aeronautical Information Services—methods for the collection and dissemination of aeronautical information required for flight operations
Annex 16	Environmental Protection. Vol. I: Aircraft Noise—specifications for aircraft noise certification, noise monitoring, and noise exposure units for land-use planning; Vol. II: Aircraft Engine Emissions—standards relating to vented fuel and emissions certification requirements
Annex 17	Security—specifications for safeguarding international civil aviation against acts of unlawful interference
Annex 18	Safe Transport of Dangerous Goods by Air—specifications for the labeling, packing, and shipping of dangerous cargo
Annex 19	Safety Management

Remotely Piloted Aircraft Systems and *ICAO Cir 328: Unmanned Aircraft Systems (UAS)*. While both documents explain a framework for the approach that state regulatory programs should undertake when looking to integrate unmanned aircraft systems into their national, and international, airspaces, *Cir 328* looks at the issues and problems facing UAS integration from a macro-conceptual level while the *Manual on Remotely Piloted Aircraft Systems* outlines very specific recommendations for personnel, operations, and training. Both approaches are vital to understanding the international governance of UAS in the long term and will be examined in this chapter.

ICAO Circular AN/328

ICAO Circular AN/328 was published in 2011 in recognition of a need to understand what ICAO's role would be in putting forth Standards and Recommended Practices (SARPS) to member states regarding Unmanned Aircraft Vehicles (UAVs). While ICAO approaches the role of UAVs as an extension of manned aviation practices, many member states present had never encountered the use of UAS or did not expect UAS to have the eventual impact seen today. This is but one reason why an exploration of UAS in AN/328 is so vital in the development of UAS regulatory systems throughout the world.

ICAO leads the international field of aviation in determining best practices and providing guidance for all nations. What is less recognized, especially in the United States and other highly developed nations, is that there exist a number of nations with minimal resources to allocate toward the safe harmonization and operation of aviation activities. Throughout Africa, Asia, and South America, countries depend on ICAO guidance for their own domestic standard and best practices along with the world; however, these regions also require an extension of ICAO activities and attention. ICAO continuously operates to help move forward best practices and standards in these regions through initiatives that allocate resources, personnel, and training as exemplified by the *No Country left Behind* initiative (International Civil Aviation Authority 1999).

ICAO approached the UAS industry through the use and incorporation of activities of member nations and recommendations of industry consensus groups. These industry consensus groups bring together commercial, governmental, and non-governmental non-profits to provide the technical and managerial experiences and knowledge requisite to developing strategies for the UAS industry. ICAO's goal is simply stated in AN/328 as to:

> provide the fundamental international regulatory framework through Standards and Recommended Practices (SARPs), with supporting Procedures for Air Navigation Services (PANS) and guidance material, to underpin routine operation of UAS throughout the world in a safe, harmonized and seamless manner comparable to that of manned operations.

This is not an unexpected approach to unmanned aircraft systems, and it is the same approach that member nations' CAAs also took in determining the future approach of UAS activities.

The first ICAO UAS exploratory meeting had taken place in Montreal on May 23, 2006 with an objective to determine the role of ICAO in UAV regulatory development. While those in attendance did agree that ICAO had a role, the majority of technical and performance specifications and standards would not need to become ICAO SARPs (International Civil Aviation Organization 2011: 1). However, the meeting did understand the vitality of ICAO's presence in harmonization and therefore came to the conclusion that ICAO should serve as the focal point for "global interoperability and harmonization, to develop a regulatory concept, to coordinate the development of UAS SARPs, to contribute to the development of technical specification by other bodies, and to identify communications requirements for UAS activity" (International Civil Aviation Organization 2011: 2). By believing it had a role to "lead and coordinate," member nations would also be thrust into the leadership role of development, and be encouraged to cooperate internationally for the certification and approval of UAS airframes and activities. The question remained, whether ICAO would publish SARPs prior to industry consensus publication, wait for member nations to haphazardly develop and deploy their own regulatory frameworks that would later require replacement or maintenance, or promote an international standard for some, but not all, elements of the UAS.

UAS activities and authorizations have developed rapidly and the technology has iterated beyond the concept of many regulators. It is pretty clear that had ICAO acted to standardize all technological elements in 2006, those standards and practices would have become woefully out of date. International standards that become "outdated" or limit technologies and their applications must be avoided, and for this reason ICAO opted not to identify which technologies or applications are necessary for successful or authorized operations, but provided guidance as to the target qualifications or performance gradations for its member states. FAA and other member nation CAAs quickly began to follow this lead, and now the belief that performance goals and metrics allow access to airspace is the most fundamental concept in the UAS industry approvals such as the FMRA Section 333 Exemption Process, type certification process, operational (COA) approvals, and 14 CFR 107 waiver applications.

An example of this performance-based approach is in discussing and identifying the roles and responsibilities of an unmanned aircraft pilot. AN/328 recognizes that:

> Personnel licensing provides harmonization within a single airspace as well as across national and regional boundaries. The remote pilot of a UAS and the pilot of a manned aircraft have the same ultimate responsibility for the safe operation of their aircraft and therefore have the same obligation for knowledge of air law and flight performance, planning and loading, human performance, meteorology, navigation, operational procedures, principles

Table 3.2 Pilot requirements that could reflect a performance goal

What type of instruction is needed to meet "flight instruction?"	What is a level of experience?
How does someone demonstrate skill as a pilot of UAS?	Does a sports pilot license qualify someone for commercial operations on UAS?
Does a pilot flying a rotor based UAS also qualify as a fixed-wing UAS pilot?	What type of currency requirement is necessary for UAS?

of flight and radiotelephony. Both pilots must obtain flight instruction, demonstrate their skill, achieve a level of experience, and be licensed.

While this outline may seem rather specific in the requirements for a pilot—to obtain flight instruction, demonstrate skill, achieve a level of experience, and be licensed—in fact, there is no element that identifies how much experience or what licensing requirement must be met. Table 3.2 shows questions left to the member nations' CAAs that *could* have been standardized but are not specifically outlined in this document.

While this non-specificity may seem as though ICAO has "passed the buck" to the CAAs to create a regulatory framework independently, it really recognizes the need for flexible, technologically driven, regional developments that can be harmonized across industry and regional tolerance. The biggest problem that ICAO seemed to recognize when outlining the future of UAS at the international level is the complication that automation technologies will have on the basic understanding of pilot responsibilities and the role this may play in reliability, security, and liability. Beyond responsibilities:

> Unique Human Factors, including sensory deprivation or motions inconsistent with the aircraft being piloted, may place unique physical or mental demands on the remote pilot. Some remote pilots may only be required and trained for takeoff/launch and landing/recovery. Other remote pilots may only need to be trained for en-route flight responsibilities excluding takeoffs and landings.

Clearly, ICAOs members that were involved in this report understand that UAS technologies may not even fit the paradigm of traditional aviation. While the concept of pilot in command can be stretched to include many pilots in one operation—similarly to modern trans-Pacific flights in commercial and military flights—the realization that any number of pilots operating thousands of miles away from the aircraft and in different countries than the actual aircraft in flight is daunting and complicates this definition.

Technology development is moving so rapidly that regulators who have never been known to be particularly quick and adaptable face an even greater challenge than ever before. As stated in AN/328:

Technologies are continuously evolving in both manned and unmanned aviation. Automation plays an ever-increasing role, particularly in transport category aircraft. Automation systems are already capable of operating the controls, keeping the aircraft on course, balancing fuel use, transmitting and receiving data from various ground facilities, identifying conflicting traffic and providing resolution advisories, plotting and executing optimum descent profiles and in some cases even taking off or landing the aircraft. The pilot is of course, monitoring all of these activities . . . A key factor in safely integrating UAS in non-segregated airspace will be their ability to act and respond as manned aircraft do. Much of this ability will be subject to technology — the ability of the aircraft to be controlled by the remote pilot, to act as a communications relay between remote pilot and air traffic control (ATC), the performance (e.g. transaction time and continuity of the communications link) as well as the timeliness of the aircraft's response to ATC instructions. Performance-based SARPs may be needed for each of these aspects.

Essentially, ICAO recognizes that automation will change the way we conceptualize aircraft operations and this will drive programmatic, managerial, and personnel changes unforeseen to date. Only through performance-based standards, rather than technologically specific standards, can any meaningful regulatory framework be created.

The greatest contribution, widely seen as a foundational document in the development of harmonized standards for unmanned aircraft systems, is this notion of performance-based goals that member nations can codify in their own time, and through their own mechanisms, to foster technological growth while maintaining safe skies for manned and unmanned operations. Without this foundation, member nations would be forced to meet specific technological inclusions in UAS, provide trainings that may or may not be appropriate, or create their own performance goals that are not harmonized internationally. This would create an otherwise difficult and extremely disjointed international airspace regime for UAS while creating any number of conflicts.

Unfortunately, ICAO in 2011 seems to have misjudged where and when the major growth of unmanned systems would take place. From AN/328, ICAO believes that "the RPA civil market is expected to develop incrementally, with usage increasing as confidence in RPA safety and reliability grows, as SARPs and technical specifications are developed, and public and industry confidence grows." What has actually occurred is that these systems have proliferated exponentially, driven by public interest and new use case development in commercial and recreational applications, not because of an increase in reliability or standardization across systems. At this point, the naiveté of regulators with a penchant for using similar industries as an example for expected results shows in how ICAO envisioned the growth of remotely piloted aircraft (RPA). Where ICAO believed that this industry would grow incrementally, it has grown exponentially and has led to a feeling of great urgency among regulators, operators, and manufacturers all seeking to minimize uncertainty in their marketplace and adopt practices that will last.

Of course ICAO is not the only organization designating standards and best practices internationally. In fact, ICAO relies upon its member organizations to create the more specific regulatory environment for operators and manufacturers. If we think of these relationships in terms of more well-understood business relationships, we see it is very similar to corporate hierarchies. ICAO sets the institutional goals and leadership requirements for the international community much like a chief executive officer or C-suite level manager. Vice-Presidents (VPs) and upper management are left to interpret these goals and objectives and translate that information into "standards" for *shalls* and *shoulds* or "best practices" for *mays* for the rest of the organization. Civil Aviation Authorities for individual member states such as the FAA or member nations' groupings of responsible state entities such as the European Aviation Safety Agency (EASA) are examples of the international aviation community's Vice-Presidents. These "Vice-Presidents" talk to their organizational leaders to determine what each organization requires and how best to achieve these "standard practices." The relationship that exists between these VPs and the C-Level at ICAO only works so far, as the VPs sit in on ICAO meetings, are represented in developing guiding documents, and help develop the leadership strategies that are published. From there, "standards and best practices," hopefully well-aligned between organizations (member nations), disseminate through nations and create a harmonious industry basis for regulations. The VP elements—the member nations' aviation regulatory bodies—pass regulations in support of those international goals (best practices—may/should) and requirements (standards—shall/must).

The following case studies show how these different organizations interact with one another in a non-United States specific example. As discussed, ICAO develops the international leadership and standards that they deem necessary for ensuring the continued development of the highest level of aviation safety and it is up to member nations to meet those standards and adopt the best practices as deemed in the Chicago Convention and Annex systems. The following case study looks at one regional player in the aviation safety community and one that is responsible for a very large, multinational body with differing interests and dramatically varying cultural approaches to economics. The other element of this case study examines an aviation rule-making committee that is more multinational in nature and works to represent all aviation authorities. These two organizations—the European Aviation Safety Association and the Joint Authorities for Rulemaking of Unmanned Systems (JARUS)—provide great examples for how that VP level of aviation interacts with the C-Level at ICAO—they provide the forum for research, guidance, and recommendations for standards and best practices through, between, and for ICAO and member nations.

The European Aviation Safety Agency (EASA)

The European Aviation Safety Agency (EASA) is the aviation safety agency recognized by the European Union, and responsible for ensuring a high and uniform level of safety in civil aviation through the adoption and implementation of safety rules and measures (Skybrary 2014). Originally this responsibility was delegated to the Joint Aviation Authorities (JAA) which ceased operation in June 30, 2009. It is important to recognize that this is not a direct replacement for this organization because the reporting structure is different from JAA and the JAA had had no real power to implement its codifications of aviation safety. JAA had relied solely on national aviation authorities (NAAs) to adopt the recommendations set to them by JAA. Realizing how impotent this structure was—similar to the American experience of the original Articles of Confederation—the European Union adopted *Regulation (EC) 216/*2008 of the European Parliament and Council in 2002. EASA has the ability to use the NAAs to implement the Regulations it has developed and provide civil penalties when entities are in non-compliance; similarly, to the United States' FAA regulatory powers.

This empowerment has gone a very long way in promoting aviation safety throughout Europe and has enabled EASA to engage the international community in creating regionally directed unmanned systems regulations. Table 3.3 illustrates EASA's responsibilities and tasks.

Table 3.3 EASA proposed responsibilities and tasks

Responsibilities

Expert advice to the EU on the drafting of new legislation

Safety analysis and research

Developing, implementing and monitoring safety rules

Type-certification of aircraft and components and approval of organizations involved in design, manufacture, and maintenance

Certification of personnel and organizations

Certification of organizations providing pan-European ATM/ANS services

Certification of organizations located outside the territory subject to EC law and responsible for providing ATM/ANS services or ATCO training in the Member States where EC applies

Authorization of Third-Country (non-EU) operators

Tasks

Help the Community legislature draw up common standards to ensure the highest possible levels of safety and environmental protections

Ensure that they are applied uniformly in Europe and that any necessary safeguard measures are implemented

Promote the spread of standards worldwide

The Responsibilities and Tasks of EASA are very similar to those granted to the FAA through legislative empowerment. They represent non-specific roles that EASA can serve when delegated rulemaking authority by the European Council. This delegation of responsibility must be in line with what is known as the "Basic Regulation" or Regulation (EC) No 216/2008 of the European Parliament and the Council of February 20, 2008 (The European Commission 2016). The agency is also bound to follow a structured rulemaking process found in Article 52(1) of this Basic Regulation, but is beyond the scope of this case study. Suffice it to say that the rulemaking procedure requires involvement from industry stakeholders—including entities such as JARUS and NAA representing member nations.

The evolution of integration efforts with unmanned aircraft internationally follows a similar story to the one in the United States of America. In the United States, as described previously, the FAA released *Roadmaps* and presented ideas for UAS integration as it was developing their NRPM of Final Rules for sUAS. A difference exists, however, in the approach to UAS classification and adoption of recommendations throughout the industry. EASA seems to be following a very different approach in that they have created regulatory guidance for all levels of UAS while the FAA has been content in creating entry classification rules for only small UAS. In the United States, larger categories of UAS require type certification or certification through another method (public use for example).

EASA's approach relies upon three main categories of UAS: Open, Specific, and Certified. These terms did not simply appear for the first time in their published Advanced Notice of Proposed Amendment 2015-10: Introduction of a regulatory framework for the operation of drones (European Aviation Safety Agency 2015). This concept of multiple classifications of unmanned aircraft had been debated from day one. The idea behind these three varying categories based on risk, is that this regulatory exercise is "not simply transposing the system put in place for manned aviation but creating one that is proportionate, progressive, risk based and . . . [expressing] objectives that will be complemented by industry standards" (European Aviation Safety Agency 2015). By understanding that risk is a vital component of the regulatory classifications of UAS, EASA seemed ahead of the FAA until the 2015/2016 roadmap update where FAA has fully adopted a risk-based approach to UAS classification and operations.

By approaching the adoption and integration of UAS into the international airspace environment, EASA set up three categories of aircraft by which they would be operationally accepted. These three categories, their responsibilities and characteristics can be seen in Table 3.4.

An early version of this regulatory process, found in the EASA Concept of Operations for Drones, illustrates the above responsibilities and risk associations expected to be codified by EASA in 2015 and the later published *A-NPA 2015–10*. This earlier document recognized that for an "Open Category" certain limitations should exist that enable "very low risk drone operations, therefore

Table 3.4 EASA categories for unmanned aircraft systems

Category	Limitations	Characteristics
Open	Should not require an authorization by an NAA Operationally limited by statute Amendment process possible beyond those limitations	Low associated risk Non-complex systems with low kinetic energy associated with the system Direct VLOS 25kgs or less No flights in "no-drone zones" No flights above 150m No flights above more than 12 people
Specific	Requires a risk assessment that will lead to an Operational Authorization in cooperation with an NAA	Medium risk associated with the aircraft type, equipment, or operation High-speed or larger mass
Certified	High(er) associated risk operations By request from organizations providing services commercially	Higher risk operations (Over people, BVLOS, fully-autonomous) High-energy vehicles

without involvement of Aviation Authorities, even for commercial operations" (European Aviation Safety Agency 2015: 3). This would also require no airworthiness approval and "no approval for licenses for operations and pilots." To qualify for Open Category under this vision, the drone must be flown under visual line of sight: 500m, at an altitude not exceeding 150m above the ground or water, and outside of specified reserved areas (airport, environmental, security). This recommendation seems to imply that an Open Category enables commercial operations without any form of pilot certification or license. This is a fundamental difference between the FAA regulatory environments for sUAS commercial operations by enabling non-certified pilots the ability to do commercial work using sUAS. While this may change soon, as Congress may force the FAA to develop a micro-UAS category that does not require licensing as a direct result of interest group involvement at the federal level, all other documentation has pointed to a license requirement—including 14 CFR 107.

Moving up the risk category spectrum, the specific category of operations is designed to provide those operations that start "posing more significant aviation risks to persons overflown or involves sharing the airspace" with other stakeholders (European Aviation Safety Agency 2015: 4). EASA's approach to this category is similar to how the FAA approaches current commercial operations in the United States for sUAS—by requiring a risk assessment and identification of mitigation measures that must be approved by the CAA. This risk assessment process must "address airworthiness, operating procedures and environment, competence of involved personnel and organizations as well as airspace issues." This next category clearly requires much more thought and experience before acceptance by the CAA in its use, and therefore symbolizes an understanding of increased risk in operational applications of UAS.

A risk assessment that returns an unacceptable level of risk to society generally, or aviation safety specifically, must also have a means to become compliant, and a benchmark of appropriate safety must be known. This is the thought behind developing a *Minimum Level of Safety* or *Equivalent Level of Safety*. EASA allows for the specific category to exist in higher-risk operations or with capabilities that may be compromised by building into their application for assessment the opportunity to provide either operational or systematic mitigations. These could include adding a ballistic parachute, an extra battery, not flying over important infrastructure, providing pilots with adequate training, or requiring a certain number of hours before flying for commercial gains. As they say, "the airworthiness assessment is closely linked to the operational environment and procedures."

EASA also delineates, in A–NPA 2015-10, the following elements of a risk assessment that must be included in order for an entity to be considerate of all aviation safety concerns and to be compliant with their proposals:

1. Area of operation: Population density, areas with special protection.
2. Airspace: Class of airspace, segregation, ATC procedures.
3. Design of the drone: Functions provided, redundancy and safety features.
4. Type of drone operation: Operational procedures.
5. Pilot competence.
6. Organizational factors of the operator.

The specific category of operations is quite simply the largest and most recognized approach to UAS for commercial entities and is the most analogous to the operational environment in the United States. The Section 333 Exemption Process accompanying the Certification of Authorization or Waivers (COA) was the FAA's mechanism for providing commercial entities operational approval while ensuring that risk is well mitigated. This method continues similarly through the 14 CFR 107 waiver process.

The final category described by the EASA in their foundational document and then cited in the A–NPA 2015-10 is the Certified Category which provides access to operations where "aviation risks rise to a level akin to normal manned aviation" (European Aviation Safety Agency 2015: 5). These operations include extremely large or fast aircraft flying at high altitudes. Some discussion has been made as to whether this category should be combined with the specific category as there could be "no upper limit" to the previous category. EASA chose to divide it to show that with greater aviation risk comes greater responsibility up to and perhaps beyond the requirements of manned aviation if an *Equivalent Level of Safety* is degraded and requiring additional processes. As EASA recognizes, the type certification process for manned aviation does not directly apply to the unmanned aviation system and new procedures or requirements for aircraft and control station, or combination type certification may be necessary.

Most recently, EASA put forth the equivalent of the FAA sUAS Notice of Proposed Rule Making (NPRM), known as the A-NPA 2015-10. This document formalized EASA's regulatory framework for unmanned aircraft integration for its member nations. The core concept defining the regulatory approach is one that is familiar to those who understand the ICAO approach. EASA designated that:

> the categories have been established with the idea that a start-up company would start to operate in the "open" category with small and simple drones in operating conditions that pose very low risk, e.g. Visual Line of Sight (VLOS) and very low altitude operations, and as its experience increases to move more progressively to the "specific" and "certified" category with more complex operations, e.g. heavier and more complex drones and Beyond Visual Line of Sight (BVLOS) operations.
>
> (European Aviation Safety Agency 2015: 8)

EASA also outlined sub-categories for unmanned aircraft within the Open classification. The Open classification will include the following breakdown:

1.   CAT A0—"Toys" and "Mini-Drones" < 1kg.
2.   CAT A1—"Very Small Drones" < 4kg.
3.   CAT A2—"Small Drones" <25kg.

EASA also established an approach to aviation safety that defines "desired, measurable outcomes." After defining the various approaches of performance-based measures, EASA acknowledges that the two specific elements used for drones will be objective-based rulemaking and process-based rulemaking, rather than performance-standard-based rulemaking more prevalent in manned aviation. The different rulemaking approaches are defined below:

1.   *Objective-based rulemaking*: Only the objective is defined, but not the means to achieve it.
2.   *Process-based rule making*: Specific organizational requirements or processes are prescribed as enablers for a desired outcome (European Aviation Safety Agency 2015: 13).

Before looking into how the regulatory bodies such as EASA use standards bodies such as JARUS, it is important to understand that the above approaches represent the "hard law" and that they prefer to leave the "soft law" to the standardization bodies (European Aviation Safety Agency 2015: 14). These groups are tasked with identifying and providing "the means to comply with the Certification Specifications for new technologies to ensure the safety objectives are met; or provide methods to perform risk assessments" (European Aviation Safety Agency 2015: 14).

Case study: Examples of international regulations

The importance of harmonious international regulations cannot be overstated in the aviation community. While many industries can operate independently via borders, regions, or multinational treatise, and those same industries can provide varying competitive advantages to manufacturing, services, or humanitarian needs across competing nations, aviation requires a harmonious and standard environment. The world does not want nation states competing based on safety or security when it comes to aviation as they sometimes do in other markets.

Standardization across nations makes sense in theory, but in practice it is extremely difficult. The very basic needs and demands of nations are vastly different. Government structures, rulemaking entities, power-base for local and regional politicians, and even the trust in technology felt by populations varies to such a degree that rulemaking is dramatically affected. It is important for anyone looking to operate across international borders to identify what regulatory barriers exist to operating a UAS, who to approach, and even why those differences exist in order to understand institutional, cultural, and professional biases.

With this in mind, the following section is included with the international chapter to show the degree to which seemingly similar countries like Austria or the United Kingdom tailor their specific national policies. Ireland and Saudi Arabia are also included in this section as examples for how, though following ICAO recommendations, the approaches and outcomes can be vastly different. It is also very important to recognize this case study section acts as a snapshot in time and may not reflect the latest regulatory publications, but instead illustrates different approaches to the growth of the UAS industry.

Austria's categorized approach to UAS integration

On January 29, 2014, Austrian Civil Aviation Authority, Austro Control, published their core document regulating unmanned aircraft, *Airworthiness and Operational Notice Nr. 67*. This document, referred to as an AON, is the mechanism by which the Austrian government outlines who is being regulated, how they are defined, the method of approval, and when or where the approval must be proposed. This AON, defines the regulated UAS as having an operating mass up to and including 150kg and operated in Austrian territory. This is a very common definition for where the civil aviation authority for a country in Europe has responsibility, and where it does not, as the Basic Regulation for EASA retains certification responsibility of any UAS over 150kg. It's pretty simple. So long as the unmanned aircraft is under 151kg and flown within the Austrian territory, the operator must meet the technical and operational requirements as set forth in this AON.

AON 67 does outline some exceptions to this definition that opens up the lower classifications of unmanned aircraft, thus allowing smaller classes—much like EASAs Open and Specific categories—to gain access to the airspace without extensive regulation to their specifications. AON 67 includes exceptions for any "Unmanned aircraft with a maximum energy of motion up to and including 79 Joules." Essentially, any unmanned aircraft that operates at less than 79 Joules does not meet the need to be regulated and is considered safe to operate without limitation in this AON. The second exception is for any UAS that goes beyond the 150kg. For these large UAS, Austro Control has deferred its ability to regulate to a higher authority–the European Aviation Safety Agency (EASA). Finally, the third and fourth exceptions to the AON are for national defense UAS and any "model aircraft with a maximum operating mass exceeding 25kg . . . [to which] the competent authority is the Austrian Aeroclub." The definition for model aircraft is given in another document, much like the AC 91-57A for the FAA in the United States. In Austria these devices are defined as:

> flying devices not used for the purpose of national defence, that can be operated independently in direct line of sight of the pilot without additional technical aid . . . the maximum distance between the model airplane and the operator is 500m . . . and the flight is only to be conducted without any commercial interest and for recreational purpose only.
>
> (Austro Control: AOT and LSA 2014: 3)

Austro Control further breaks down the classification of UAS into Model Aircraft, Class 1, and Class 2 UAS. Table 3.5 illustrates these classifications as defined by Austro Control.

It is easy to see similarities between EASA recommended requirements for CAA, FAA approaches to operationalizing difference types of UAS, and the manner by which ICAO has approached unmanned aircraft systems. Beyond the technical components and operational limitations, Austro Control

Table 3.5 Classifications of UAS by Austro Control

Model Aircraft	Not to be used for national defence Can be operated independently in direct line of sight of the pilot Maximum distance between model airplane and operator is 500m Flight is only allowed to be conducted without any commercial interest and for recreational purposes only
Class 1	Not to be used for national defence Can be operated independently in direct line of sight of the pilot with additional technical aid Maximum distance between the unmanned aircraft and operator can exceed 500m Can be conducted for remuneration (commercial)
Class 2	Not to be used for national defence Can be operated independently without direct line of sight of the pilot

has developed a scheme for evaluating the proposal from an operator for commercial operations. The approach that Austro Control follows is likewise similar to the approach of FAA.

Austro Control established an approach that divides UAS into mass categories and environmental categories. As AON 67 points out, "An evaluation scheme is established that contemplates the mass of unmanned aircraft, environmental conditions as well as the building – and the population density." Table 3.6 breaks down these classifications further to illustrate how each element of the risk analysis contributes to operational and technical approval by Austro Control.

Table 3.6 represents Austro Control's approach to approving operations in Austria for UAS. When an unmanned aircraft weighing less than 5kg aims to operate in an undeveloped or unsettled environment as defined by AON 67, the airworthiness and approval requirements automatically trigger a "Classification A" approval process. This is the least rigorous for approval, whereas D is the most rigorous.

The less-than-5kg aircraft does not have to comply with special airworthiness requirements, a non-complex manual is sufficient, the UAS must be identifiable and assignable (registered), a pre-flight checklist has to be conducted, the UAS must be operated within specified operating limits (similar to a COA), and it must comply with Permissible Noise Levels Order (Austro Control: AOT and LSA 2014: 7). This Category A represents the very same category as the FAA UAS Part 107 sUAS flight operations. However, there are some additional requirements that have not yet been finalized, though they have been discussed, recommended, and in some cases required in the United States. These additional requirements include valid insurance, records for up to two years, and actual approval from the CAA rather than tacit approval via an overarching regulation found in 14 Code of Federal Regulations (CFR) 107.

Higher categories (B, C, D) require increased complexities of controls, mitigations for accidents or incidents when in more populated areas, formalized hazard and risk analysis such as Failure Mode and Effect Analysis (FMEA), and verifications of compliance moving up through the risk spectrum. Recall as well that this is only for UAS up to the 150kg size as anything beyond that is subject to EASA regulation.

Table 3.6 Austrian severity classifications

Mass Classifications	Area of Operations			
	Undeveloped	Unsettled	Settled	Densely Populated
Up to and including 5kg	A	A	B	C
Up to and including 25kg	A	B	C	D
Up to and including 150kg	B	C	D	D

Light UAVs in the United Kingdom

The United Kingdom, much like Austria, has outlined policies and procedures for determining the applicability of airworthiness standards and operational requirements for UAS. Originally, CAP 722 outlined the UK's approach to all UAS. However, since the formation and relegation of responsibilities to EASA, the UK found that CAP 722 would need to be reassessed for the size categories of up to and including 150kg—in the same fashion as Austria and many other European nations. On May 28, 2004, the UK Civil Aviation Authority published the "Policy for Light UAV Systems" outlining the methods that small UAVs can gain access to the national airspace.

Similar to Austro Control, the UK CAA developed a categorization methodology based on mass and operating environment, supplemented by speed to the limiting factors. Noting that due to the limitation of technologies such as sense-and-avoid capabilities, UAVs are likely to require operational constraint and segregation from manned aviation until parity between the two types of aviation is created. The UK is operating from a sense that as long as an *Equivalent Level of Safety* (ELOS) can be established for UAS and manned aviation, operational constraints will be required and it is up to both the proponents and the CAA to determine the requirements for establishing the ELOS.

As EASA is responsible for all UAS above 150kg, the UK CAA addresses this Light UAV Policy to those unmanned systems that do not exceed 150kg in take-off weight, in which an impact to the ground or air will not yield over 95kj of energy, and in which the speed in level flight will not exceed 70 knots. For those wondering, it should be noted that the capabilities to fly above 70 knots is acceptable, just the standard operating procedures and formalized procedures acknowledge no flight is allowed beyond 70 knots for the operation to be approved. Further limitations include a "standard" no flights above 400ft AGL (above ground level), and not beyond 500m from the UAV pilot. The UK CAA also identifies 7kg as the lower limit for regulation and that anything else falls to the small aircraft definition thereby exempting them from most regulations.

The Light UAV Policy is an interesting and expansive document in that it explains through example some of these limitations, and affords flexibility to the above constraints. Take for example the knowledge that if speed goes down, mass can go up when calculating a limiting impact transfer. It would be disingenuous, then, to say that the speed of 70 knots would always offer the same safety concern without regard to weight. With this in mind, the UK CAA included Appendix 1 in their document—Table 3.7, entitled "The Relationship between Mass and Maximum Level Speed." This table illustrates how mass and speed are interrelated in kinetic energy calculation for approval by the CAA. This has become known as the kinetic energy spectrum and much of the current regulatory thought with relation to UAS safety is based on this type of understanding.

Table 3.7 Kinetic energy calculations for UAS flight categorizations

Mass of UAV kg	Maximum speed in level flight (Vmax) Knots	1.4 Vmax M/S	Kinetic energy at 1.4 Vmax KJ
60	70	50	76
70	70	50	89
75	70	50	95
80	68	49	95
90	64	46	95
100	60	44	95
110	58	42	95
120	55	40	95
130	53	38	95
140	51	37	95
150	49	36	95

It is easy to see that the UK CAA put together this table to help applicants understand the relationship between mass and speed quickly, to facilitate the application process in a more open manner.

While there are other elements of the UK UAS regulatory environment, much of it can be found with little interpretation requisite in UK CAP 722. The reader is encouraged, if operating in the UK, to examine this document thoroughly. Much of the information is similar to the FAA or ICAO approach to UAS safety and operation and therefore left out here.

A more relaxed approach in Ireland?

The Irish approach to regulating UAS activity in its airspace has been less quantitative in nature than other examples. Interestingly, Ireland's UAS policy takes great pains to outline their compliance and deference to ICAO and EASA regulations and to identify clearly where the EASA oversight is limited to ensure Ireland's own regulatory responsibilities are well defined within the context of international obligations. While other nations in a similar position have taken great pains to outline very quantitative limitations in risk acceptance, impact spread, velocity maximums, and population density, the Irish Aviation Authority (IAA) outlines responsibilities of operators and very qualitative definitions for operation and environments.

Most importantly for Irish air control, unmanned aircraft operators must understand that they are not to create undue burden on air traffic controllers and that any contact between an operator and ATC must first begin with "ATC . . . fully aware that they are dealing with an RPAS flight" (Irish Aviation Authority, Safety Regulation Division 2013). Further, any "special provisions" that are made with the associated ATC must not diminish or limit the situational awareness of the respective ATC operator. Clearly, a great focus has been put on the ability of ATC to continue to manage their airspace without any impact from UAS operations. The Irish CAA also identifies that "RPAS must be able to comply with instructions from the ATC provider and with the equipment requirements applicable to the class of airspace within which they intend to operate." The Irish CAA means to ensure that UAS have no negative safety effect on the ATC operator that is required for coordination of efforts; a somewhat unique addition to regulations in the unmanned aircraft world.

While in the United States, the FAA has outlined airport management responsibilities for approving flights within five miles of an airport (which may include heliports found at some universities, hospitals, or on top of large buildings), the method of approval for these airport managers has not been well defined. The author is currently leading an effort to outline the process by which airport management assess the risk and negative effect of such an operation in order to empower the appropriate entity with making a reasonable decision. Without clear guidance, such as found in the Irish definition—"No negative impact"—it is unclear how an airport manager should assess such an operation, or how an operator can effectively mitigate the risk to an acceptable level for decision makers.

Irish CAA requirements go on to include the standard procedures for drone operations—procedures for an RPAS Operations Manual that include take-off and landing, en-route responsibilities, loss of control data link likelihood, and abort for critical system failings (Irish Aviation Authority Safety Regulation Division 2013: 8). Of course, all RPAS must remain within line of sight and be flown in accordance to VFR conditions, they must be flown no further than 500 meters from the point of operation, at a height of no more than 400ft AGL, not above the confines of "a congested area except with the written permission of the Authority," and not operated within controlled airspace except with the written permission of the Controlling Authority (Irish Aviation Authority Safety Regulation Division 2013: 8). Beyond the "standard" operational limitations, the Irish CAA has seen fit to prevent flights within 5km of an aerodrome, operated within 150 meters laterally of an "assembly of persons" or "vessel, vehicle or structure not under the control of an aircraft operator," within 50 meters of any person during take-off or landing, and within 2km of an aircraft in flight (Irish Aviation Authority Safety Regulation Division 2013: 9). Finally, all UAS operators must have "third party liability insurance policies" that cover the operation of the system.

While many operators and companies may look at these requirements as being roughly the same as those found in the United States, one difference is stark—all these requirements do not differ between commercial and hobby/recreational UAS. These requirements are the same whether you are flying for fun or for work (Murphy 2014).

A kingdom's need for drones

The Kingdom of Saudi Arabia put together one of the more user-friendly regulatory engagement websites existing today for those interested in operating unmanned aircraft in their airspace. Unfortunately for operators, the ability to fly in the kingdom is somewhat more restrictive than many other nations. The United Arab Emirates (UAE) published CAR *Part VIII Subpart 10* through the General Civil Aviation Authority (GCAA) governing all aviation activities in the kingdom. The approach the GCAA took to UAS is the most restrictive for individuals/hobbyists and more enabling to commercial and government needs. This is a very different approach from the United States, where privacy concerns and freedom of flight have much stronger constituencies having an effect on policy. In the United States, there is much greater power by "rights" groups that are concerned with privacy invasion, law enforcement use, and commercial responsibilities to the public which has led directly to greater freedom for hobbyists than for commercial or law enforcement needs. Without discussing too much again the commercial vs individual flight rules, it is much more difficult to fly a small drone in the United States for commercial gains than for individual use. Such is not the case in the UAE.

The GCAA divides unmanned aircraft operations into three main categories based on weight, with each main category divided into two sub-categories based on usage. The small end of the weight spectrum (Categories 1 and 2) are divided into private and individual use and commercial or state use. Table 3.8, copied from the GCAA RPAS webpage, shows how the UAE GCAA has divided classifications of UAS (United Arab Emirates General Aviation Authority 2015).

The category designations for UAS are very different from those identified by EASA and other institutions. While the 5kg and less, and the 5kg–25kg environments are similar to the EASA rules for Category A1 and A2 (4kg and 25kg respectively for EASA), the determination that anything above 25kg follow the same regulatory pathway is very different (European Aviation Safety Agency 2015). Similarly, the distinction between commercial, state, and private or individual use is different in their interpretation of who can gain access to the airspace.

The GCAA also included the following distinctions for UAS operating in the UAE. Their understanding of weight and type of use is somewhat outdated as most other CAAs have adopted risk-based classifications that take into account Concept of Operations, population density of operation, and other important factors discussed previously. Based on the category system, private/individual users have the following unique requirements in addition to standard requirements witnessed through other sections (no flights above 400ft, within 5km of an aerodrome, not near buildings, houses or private property, etc.).

These requirements seem to go above and beyond the state of other nations; however they are only for those private/individuals. Looking at the commercial

Table 3.8 Categories for individual and private use UAS in the UAE

Category 1	< 5kg	Use of any kind of video or image capturing device on UAS/drone is prohibited UAS/drone equipped to drop or release any item is prohibited Not allowed to fly over public or private properties Frequency restrictions (29.7 – 47.0 MHz, max power 10mW, or 2400 – 2500 MHz max power 100 mW) If a pilot sees or hears a manned aircraft the drone must land immediately Security clearance required regardless of payload
Category 2	5kg > 25kg	The applicant must file a form to purchase the UAS/drone through GCAA licensing department No video or image capturing device Only flight within flying club or allocated zone Frequency restrictions (29.7 – 47.0 MHz, max power 10mW, or 2400 – 2500 MHz max power 100 mW) Security clearance required regardless of payload
Category 3	25kg <	Not permitted in controlled airspace Same restrictions above Security clearance required before permission of ANY operation

entities looking to fly in the UAE, they are able to capture images and data via UAS/drone use, and have access to large areas through the approval process of the UAE. Specifically, commercial and government entities looking to operate for survey, aerial work, petroleum, firefighting, media, air shows, agriculture, screening, weather forecasting, wildlife protection, and surveillance can expect expedited approval process.

From the outside, it is clear that the GCAA is encouraging the growth and application of the UAS industry commercially while remaining unsure about the implications of that same industry for personal and private activities. Privacy concerns and individual "spying" seem to be at the top of the list of drone concerns for the GCAA limiting the personal use of drones within the country.

Table 3.9 shows the full categorization of UAS activities for UAE and is included to illustrate the differences in approach between commercial and state run operations, and private or individual operations.

Table 3.9 Commercial and state use for UAS in the UAE

Category	Mass	Restrictions and requirements
1	< 5kg	User manual must be strictly adhered to
		Do not endanger people or property
		Give way to other aircraft
		Land when another aircraft is sighted
		GCAA permission is required for using camera or scanning or surveillance equipment
		UAS registration
		E-Service UAs operating approval
		Security approval for camera
2	5kg > 25kg	Same as above
3	25kg <	Same as above

4 Domestic regulations, standards and the FAA roadmap

The Federal Aviation Administration became the sole entity responsible for overseeing and regulating the national airspace for commercial aircraft for the United States in the Federal Aviation Act of 1958 (FAA 2015). It quickly became the leader in safety promotion and regulation in aviation, and for decades represented the unparalleled experts in the industry. Since its inception, civil aviation throughout the world has modeled their operations, standards, regulations, and structure after Federal Aviation Administration leadership—only recently has ICAO taken the mantle in safety theory and accident prevention. The success of the FAA's oversight region cannot be overstated. Most recently, ICAO identified North America as the "only UN region to have 0 fatal crashes [commercial passenger category] and as the second lowest in accident rates for the year." Applying this same level of success to the unmanned aircraft is a difficult task; yet that is precisely what has been asked of the administration. The FAA has been responsible for the managing of airspace access for over 50 years and it has now been tasked by Congress to integrate unmanned aircraft safely and securely.

Legislation mandating full integration of UAS into the national airspace first appeared within the FAA Modernization and Reform Act of 2012 H.R. 658—a highly politicized act passed late in the term of President Obama's 2008–2012 term in office. The context and political environment within which this act was passed matters greatly in understanding the political environment in which the UAS industry finds itself currently and to understand the levels of funding for government operations. This act is an appropriations and guidance document that delineates the powers given to the FAA, offers direction for projects to be undertaken by the FAA, and provides funding for those projects. It is within this act that funding and direction are very important in determining the resources authorized by the executive and legislative branches of federal government to the appropriate administrative branch of government—the Federal Aviation Administration. Not until June 21, 2016 was the first regulation regarding sUAS published, and even that regulation was not enforceable until August 2016.

H.R. 658 was a joint Act of Congress that included a great deal of aviation related issues, especially relating to the upgrading of outdated aviation systems and movement toward the NextGen Airspace. The aspects of the act most important to the UAS industry can be found in Title I, Sec. 104 and Sec. 105 for funding allowances and Title III, Sec. 331–Sec. 336 as they outline all UAS related legislation (U.S. Congress, House of Representatives 2012). Title III is a section dealing with safety responsibilities and definitions. It is within this Title that the UAS integration into the national airspace has been included, and within which the UAS Roadmap we discuss later is outlined. This Act of Congress was signed on February 14, 2012 immediately following furlough days for FAA employees and contractors the previous Fall (Elias, Brass and Kirk 2013). Near to picketing, the FAA was forced into agreeing to short-term concessions after losing a somewhat quiet media war, whereby opposition to FAA funding increases called the FAA "selfish" as "flights were missed, safety put at risk, and the public at large in danger." With Congress looking at a massive deficit moving into an election year, it became difficult to warrant the expanded funding of new projects—especially publicly scrutinized projects clouded along partisan lines (Congressional Business Office 2013: 18). This explains the lack of funding as political leaders scrutinized every dollar allotted to their constituency's questionable programs. Combining a contentious topic that was publicly questioned with no funding and even less institutional eagerness to take on an amorphous new technology for regulations, it is no wonder that the FAA seemed hindered in initial attempts to regulate the industry.

Further hampering the work to certify and include UAS into the national airspace were "anti-big government" groups seeking to leverage public concerns about privacy against attempts to move toward autonomous and human-in-the-loop UAS variances. The general public in the United States has been very outspoken in concern for privacy violations and this continues to influence the national debate and funding efforts of Federal Aviation Administration. These concerns immediately led every pro-integration group to issue responses to the privacy concerns. As anyone that is familiar with debate, once an issue has warranted a response, let alone a large response from every major stakeholder, it becomes a legitimate topic of debate. We only need to look so far as the most recent political elections in the United States and United Kingdom. Once an attack has been made, and in turn a response warranted, the initial attack is seen as having weight and truth behind it. In this way, the privacy concerns against UAS were adopted as a banner for all anti-UAS, anti-technology advancement groups looking for reasons why drones were bad.

Representing more than 7,000 members and 22,000 organizations as well as 66 nations, the Association for Unmanned Vehicle Systems International (AUVSI)—the leading lobbyist in the UAS industry—issued the following comments:

> AUVSI supports the expanded use of unmanned systems, and believes unmanned systems can be used lawfully and responsibly without infringing upon Constitutional rights . . . AUVSI believes there is already a robust

legal framework to allow UAS to operate without infringing upon Constitutional rights that protect privacy, and that this framework is applicable and sufficient to guide the use of systems operated from the ground.

Many involved in the UAS industry believe in this approach to privacy—that identifying the "tried and true" legal framework governing helicopter surveillance and other forms of aviation-based surveillance would be enough.

The roadmap moving forward for UAS had been ambitious, as industry leaders and stakeholders continue to push for greater understanding of the process. Very important questions needed to be answered expeditiously and only through the development of clear and concise regulations could, and can, this take place. Though advocates for this blossoming technology called for a quickened pace and less regulation, they would be the same individuals damaged by an otherwise avoidable incident due to lack of established guidelines; many agencies realized this and only the most irresponsible voices continue to bemoan the pace of integration. This is where domestic private–public partnership groups such as RTCA and ASTM entered into the equation— leveraging highly specialized expertise into regulatory recommendations for the FAA. Partnerships between private companies (Boeing, Lockheed Martin, Raytheon, Aerovironment), Academia (University of Southern California, North Dakota State University, Embry-Riddle University), and government agencies (NASA, FAA, TSA, Army, Navy, Air Force) allow leaders in the fields of business and research to partner with the regulatory and legislative leadership to produce supportive standards for government created regulations. These standards are often referred to as industry consensus standards and their roots can be found in the Administrative Procedures Act (APA).

Federal regulations evolve over time reflecting changes in support, public opinion, and technology that affect the questions of safety, need, and supply of emerging technologies. In the case of unmanned aircraft systems the regulatory scheme outlining the appropriate and safe use within the civil airspace system continues to change very rapidly. Federal policy decisions began in 2005 with the most significant addition occurring through the Federal Aviation Administration Modernization and Reform Act of 2012. Much changed between 2005 and this legislative act. Where once the FAA determined that "COA applications for civil UA operations will not be accepted," just one year later they agreed that "approvals for both COA and special airworthiness certificates . . . depends on whether the applicant is a civil user or a public user . . . public applicants should utilize the COA application process . . . Civil applicants must apply for the airworthiness certificate."

The first document outlining the operations and methods for acquiring certification within the national airspace for unmanned aircraft system was AFS-400 UAS Policy 05-01, published September 16, 2005, from the Federal Aviation Administration. This first document is a response to the question of whether UAS operation will "be allowed to conduct flight operations in the

U.S. National Airspace System (NAS)." Without issuing particular legislation for civil access, the policy publication looked into ramifications of NAS integration relating to national security, industry background, and lists important definitions necessary for discussing the issues at hand while beginning to outline a framework for certification access.

AFS-400 identified that "it has become necessary to develop guidance for Federal Aviation Administration organization to use when evaluating application for Certificate(s) of Waiver or Authorization." It begins by outlining the challenges to civil aviation—problems that are still faced in developing cogent regulatory framework and systems design as, ". . . considerable work is ongoing to develop certifiable 'detect, sense and avoid' system . . . an acceptable solution to the 'see and avoid' problem for UA." To this day, sense-and-avoid (SAA) or detect-and-avoid (DAA), are still to blame for a lack of integration into all airspace. Once the technological hurdles of SAA/DAA are overcome, there will be much greater adoption as the safety question will be much better answered.

What we see in later documents is a frequently used method of allowing unlike technologies to co-exist using the same formative language in regulations as *equivalent levels of safety*. Equivalent levels of safety allow a designer to certificate a system using proof that a system meets a level of safety used for other like systems, but without the same method of demonstration, often because the intrinsic nature of the technology will not allow for the same standard for certification. An example of this, identified in this early FAA publication, is given in acknowledging that if:

> UA operators were held rigorously to the "see and avoid" requirements of Title 14, Code of Federal Regulation (14 CFR) part 91.1131, Right-of-Way Rules, there would be no UA flights in civil airspace . . . the FAA supports UA flight activities that can demonstrate that the proposed operations can be conducted by an acceptable level of safety.
>
> (FAA 2005)

The final framework being established in this early guiding document is that the FAA allows that, ". . . acceptable system safety studies must include a hazard analysis, risk assessment, and other appropriate documentation that support the 'extremely improbable' determination" for certificating UAS (FAA 2005). This naming of "extremely improbable" is not a meaningless definition for risk assessment, but comes with a quantitative probability that is reduced to the point where a systems engineer can deem a failure "extremely improbable." This definition is associated with a probability of occurrence per operational hour less than 1×10^{-9}, or, "so unlikely that it is not anticipated to occur during the entire operational life of an entire system or fleet." Creating a mitigation system that enables UAS to exhibit a level of safety equivalent to manned aircraft is the crux of integration efforts. Only when these safety requirements are equivalent and able to be proven in a system agnostic manner will integration be successful.

If we take a moment to consider the current conditions of UAS integration, we see efforts to provide a "mini-UAS" category access to national airspace without concern of a likelihood of incident. The belief is that, because the possible kinetic energy (KE) that could be created by a mini-UAS (less than 4.4 lb) striking another object is so low, the corresponding risk level of that accident does not require all regulatory protections accorded to other weight categories (U.S. Congress 2016). While this legislative effort may have merit, and there has been preliminary research outlining that in fact the occurrence of mid-air collision (the greatest worry for aviation safety) is so low, that there is little need for greater protections against even drone strikes weighing less than 55lb. What both Congress and a Mercatus Center policy report fail to realize is that weight is only half of the equation when considering potential severity for an in-flight collision. When determining KE, the formula describes the characteristics of kinetic energy at any one point. Looking at the equation we see that though mass of an object is very important, the kinetic energy follows speed exponentially. Therefore, the greater the speed the higher the kinetic energy to a much more significant degree than weight. Neither the micro-UAS legislation nor the Mercatus Center policy briefing consider speed when discussing the risk. The Mercatus Center publication also raises concerns regarding the impact that interest group funded research and biases play on the type of research being conducted in the UAS industry. I wish it were true that we could say with all honesty bird strike data can be extrapolated to drone mishap or incident data in the way Dorrado and Hammond describe. Their biases, for anyone looking closely enough, require scrutiny as Mercatus Center is considered one of the most right-wing, anti-government regulation Think Tanks in the United States. Its very name—Mercatus—means "free market." It's important for a research institution to be understood for what it is, highly biased toward reducing regulations. Sometimes that means flawed research design as is the case here.

In 2006, Kenneth Davis, Manager of the Unmanned Aircraft Program Office within the Federal Aviation Administration, issued a "notice of policy; opportunity for feedback" memorandum delivering guidance and explanation for AFS-400 UAS Policy 05-01. For roughly a year there had been confusion as to the method by which unmanned aircraft would gain access to the national airspace, if at all, and whether an equivalent level of safety may be allowed indefinitely. This policy memo addressed the following: "Regulatory standards need to be developed to enable current technology for unmanned aircraft to comply with Title 14 Code of Federal Regulations (CFR)." It also goes on to define concepts unique to unmanned aircraft, such as pilot in command (PIC). With manned aircraft, the PIC was always the pilot and that individual had features that are often taken for granted.

1. A personal investment in the safety of the plane as an extension of person safety.

2. Sensory feedback and avoidance maneuvers without mediation of latency and other connectivity issues.

The FAA recognizes that these two changes matter immensely in the safe use and certification of UAS as they lack both defined characteristics of manned aircraft. Manned aircraft certifications and access as well as training use both features for safety and normal use; thus an equivalent level of safety has to be considered for certifying UAS rather than relying upon current 14 CFR Part 91 regulations. Davis goes on to argue:

> The FAA guidance supports unmanned aircraft flight activity that can be conducted at an acceptable level of safety . . . [where] the operator is required to establish the Unmanned Aircraft System's (UAS) airworthiness either from FAA certification, a DoD airworthiness statement, or by other approved means.

This is the first time that certifications from other entities, or other manners of certification more in line with manned aviation, have been brought into the discussion as an alternative to full integration for Certificate of Authorization modalities. It begins the guiding principle that Aerovironment has been able to acquire commercial licensing—using the special airworthiness certificate process (Federal Aviation Administration 2014).

This same guiding policy document, written in reference to AFS-400 UAS Policy 05-01, mentions the importance of advancing UAS technology into the national airspace. Davis sees unmanned aircraft having "a variety of uses in the public section, their application in commercial or civil use is equally diverse . . ." and that it is a "quickly growing and important industry." Finally, Davis acknowledges that, "the current FAA policy for UAS operations is that no person may operate a UAS in the National Airspace System without . . . specific authority . . ." and that ". . . for UAS operating as public aircraft the authority is the COA, for UAS operating as civil aircraft the authority is special airworthiness certificates, and for model aircraft the authority is AC 91-57." These statements are the foundation for the way the FAA has approached integrating UAS in to the NAS. It began with the FAA disallowing all UA for civil, but not public, use. It outlined methods that would, for a short time, continue to grow the UA industry and give signs that access would be granted for civil purposes. The next step would come in 2008 with an updated vision statement and a more in-depth delineation of responsibilities within the FAA. Also, an expansion of allowed activity for UAS is notable in language and procedure running the gamut of airspaces.

While these policy memos did show an evolving interpretation of UAS and began to provide a foundation for FAA involvement in regulating, it does not actually create a regulatory framework by which enforcement of these policies existed. As we will discuss later, the courts have had difficulty empowering the FAA to enforce their guidelines that are evolving at this time. The FAA, though providing insight and guidance to UA operators and manufacturers, seemed to be doing so in a completely—according to some courts—voluntary manner.[5] These guidances are internal in nature and therefore do not replace the need for substantial regulations that are American Procedures Act compliant.

The next formative policy document, published by the Aviation Safety Unmanned Aircraft Program Office AIR-160 on March 13, 2008, came in the form of *Interim Operational Approval Guidance 08-01: Unmanned Aircraft Systems Operations in the U.S. National Airspace System*. This would stand longer than the previous two until the next regulatory document in 2012 FRMA. AIR-160 built upon the previous policy guidance; however, it moved beyond them and developed the regulatory outlook by which the UAS NAS integration scheme would begin to develop. From the beginning, the document gives profoundly better reasoning as to the need for special regulations for UAS. By acknowledging that a large number of applications for special certifications for UAS operations are being sought as a direct result of "the fact that unmanned aircraft (UA) are not compliant with various sections of Title 14 of the Code of Federal Regulations (14 CFR) and therefore, require an alternate means of compliance . . ." as caused ". . . most notably [by] the lack of an on-board pilot require[ing] an alternate method of the 'see and avoid' provisions of 14 CFR 91.113, Right-of-Way Rules: Except Water Operations." It goes on to address new challenges and elaborate upon previously identified hazards to integrating UAS into the NAS. Among these are "areas of pilot certification, crew certification, pilot currency, medical certificates, and airworthiness." Further, this document's scope is limited to only two types of approval:

1. Certificates of Waivers or Authorizations (COA).
2. Special Airworthiness Certificates.

Both are limited to non-Restricted, Prohibited or Warning Area airspace unless specifically requested by the applicant (Federal Aviation Administration AIR-160 2008: 2). Most generally, COAs were the method by which public users (federal, state, and local agencies) acquire approval for flight operations using a UA, and special airworthiness certificates the method for civil applications. This is often the confusing element for a lot of users, though today the drone community has a much better handle on the regulatory environment than it once did due to outreach efforts and continued engagement with the community.

This 2008 document continued to refine the requirements based upon airspace access and operation for non-small UAS activities. Within the 08-01 policy document, it is stated that "Unless specifically authorized, UAS operations in other than Restricted, Prohibited, or Warning Areas, or Class A airspace shall require visual observers, either airborne or ground based." You can see the consistency between documents and definitions for required flight. Realize also, that by then, three years of public work—in addition to all

Table 4.1 AIR-160 system considerations for mitigating risk in unmanned aircraft systems

Onboard cameras/sensors	May be used for sense and avoid issues as well as onboard problems that would not be detected by a sub-system such as onboard fire, icing, corrosion, payload malfunction, etc.
Radar and other sensors	May be used for sense and avoid problems associated with cooperative and non-cooperative aircraft, target with low radar reflectivity, and other operational altitudes and ranges that exhibit constant interaction with targets
Lost link procedures	In all cases, the UAS must have an automatic recovery method in the event of a lost link – the intent is "to ensure airborne operations are predictable in the event of lost link"
Flight termination system (FTS)	Must be included where a UAS is lacking in system redundancies – this would be an independent flight termination system manually controlled by the PIC

procedures and processes put in place by military operators—had gone in to developing regulations that would enable UAS to operate safely in the NAS.

The 2008 guidance by the FAA illustrated the methods by which a system can be certified for access into the NAS. While this helped to diminish uncertainty for developers, designers, and manufacturers for how to build their systems and how to address safety concerns, it did not offer a timetable for integration or lawful use of UAS. In order to show the equivalent level of safety, or any level of safety, the FAA acknowledges that:

> risk mitigation may also include other methods or systems that an applicant may propose for consideration. An applicant may propose any reasonable type of mitigation or system, however, the FAA approves UAS flight activities that can demonstrate that the proposed operations can be conducted an acceptable level of safety . . . acceptable system safety studies must include hazard analysis, risk assessment, and other appropriate documentation that support "extremely improbable" determination.
>
> (Federal Aviation Administration AIR-160 2008: 8)

The Safety Management Systems for UAS section of this publication offers a quick insight into the leading theory of aviation safety used today in airports, for Part 91 operators, mandated by ICAO, and increasingly being required by FAA. Safety Management Systems are the future of UAS safety and are currently being integrated into all six of the UAS test sites. Further, in interviews with FAA representatives, it is clear that SMS will be required by UAS operations to meet equivalent levels of safety.

The Unmanned Aircraft Program Office within the FAA became inundated with both COA and special airworthiness certificate requests and thus it is clear that permanent, well-defined regulations are necessary. Between 2005 and 2010 there had been 94 Special Airworthiness Certificates (SAC-EC) issued to 13 civil operators covering both UAS and Optionally Pilots Aircraft (OPA) (North Central Texas Regional General Aviation and Heliport Plan 2012: 20). Further, FAA issued 146 COAs in 2009 and 298 in 2010 giving a total of 251 active COAs for 77 different UAs as of June 28, 2011 (North Central Texas Regional General Aviation and Heliport Plan 2012: 21). The demand for COAs and SACs reflected a need for firm framework and safety regulations in order to continue to grow in the unmanned industry.

It is important to remember that while this document seems very recent, the proliferation of UA systems occurred recently as well. It wasn't until the Gulf War in 1991 that UASs became a staple of the US military. UA manufacturers only recently recognized the public and civil uses they had to offer in a dynamic, information technology driven society. It is essential to remember that while industry leaders such as AUVSI admonish the Federal Aviation Administration (FAA) for slow integration, and that limited access to airspace is having a negative impact on the unmanned aviation community, the movement for integration is moving relatively quickly. By identifying 2015 as the target date for publication of all UAS in the National Air Space (NAS), Congress set a very ambitious target. When one considers the scientific analysis, technological development, constituency involvement, and public distrust of drones coupled with the unrecognized push-back against government surveillance and up-swells of anti-government politics it is amazing that the FAA has been able to come as far as they have.

In its simplest form, the regulatory environment for authorized flights currently follows the flowchart developed in Figure 4.1. The flowchart illustrates the decision path for determining what type of authorization an organization needs in order to fly legally in the national airspace and is a holdover from the FMRA 2012. Remember, this is the pathway that exists to those commercial operators prior to the regulatory developments according to the newly developed 14 CFR 107 that will be discussed later. The options are differentiated upon the type of organization applying for operational approval. If an organization is part of a civil organization (government, law enforcement, military) they have the ability to self-certify their program and systems.

For the FAA this ensured that the system of flight had already been used and transferred from military use or special airworthiness certification, much like a surplus helicopter used in the military can be used by coast guard or law enforcement entities. It is also the same mechanism allowing otherwise unobtainable N numbers for military grade aircraft. This civil entity would then need to apply for operation approvals—the Certificate of Authorization or Waiver (COA)—which would identify where, how, and when an operation can take place using a UA. Non-civil entities had it much more difficult, and

Table 4.2 FAA Modernization and Reform Act of 2012 roadmap

May 14, 2012	Simplify the process of issuing COAs or waivers for public UAS	Complete
Aug. 12, 2012	Establish a program to integrate UAS into NAS at 6 test ranges	Complete
Aug. 12, 2012	Develop an Arctic UAS operation plan and initiate a process to work with relevant federal agencies communities to designate permanent areas in the arctic where small unmanned aircraft may operate 24 hours per day	Complete
Aug. 12, 2012	Determine whether certain UAS can fly safely in the NAS before the completion of the Act's requirements for a comprehensive plan and rulemaking to safely accelerate the integration of civil UAS in the NAS or the Act's requirement for issuance of guidance regarding the operation of public UAS including operating a UAS with a COA or waiver	Complete
Nov. 10, 2012	Expedite the issuance of a COA for public safety entities	Complete
Nov. 10, 2012	Develop a comprehensive plan to safely accelerate integration of civil UAS into NAS	Complete
Nov. 10, 2012	Issue guidance regarding operation of civil UAS to expedite COA process; provide collaborative process with public agencies to allow an incremental expansion of access into the NAS as technology matures and the necessary safety analysis and data become available and until standards are completed and technology issues are resolved; facilitate capability of public entities to develop and use test ranges; provide guidance on public entities' responsibility for operation	Complete
Feb. 12, 2013	Make operational at least one project at a test range	Complete
Feb. 14, 2013	Approve and make publicly available a 5-year road map for the introduction of civil UAS into NAS, to be updated annually	Complete
Feb. 14, 2013	Submit to Congress a copy of the plan	Complete
Aug. 14, 2014	Publish in the Federal Register the Final Rule on small UAS	Complete
Aug. 14, 2014	Publish in the Federal Register a Notice of Proposed Rulemaking to implement recommendation of the comprehensive plan	None to date
Aug. 14, 2014	Publish in the Federal Register an update to the Administration's Policy statement on UAS in Docket No. FAA-2006-25714	None to date
Sep. 30, 2015	Achieve safe integration of civil UAS into the NAS	In process
Dec. 14, 2015	Publish in the Federal Register a Final Rule to implement the recommendations of the comprehensive plan	None to date
Dec. 31, 2015	Develop and implement operational and certification requirements for public UAS in NAS	None to date
Feb. 14, 2017	Report to Congress on the test ranges	None to date

only after the FAA Modernization and Reform Act of 2012 included Section 333, could they take away much of the need for special airworthiness certifications.

Section 333 of the FMRA 2012 empowered them to determine:

> which types of unmanned aircraft systems, if any, as a result of their size, weight, speed, operational capability, proximity to airports and populated areas, and operation within visual line of sight do not create a hazard to users of the national airspace system or the public or pose a threat to national security; and whether a certificate of waiver, certificate of authorization, or airworthiness certification under section 44704 of title 49 . . . If the Secretary determines under this section that certain unmanned aircraft systems may operate safely in the national airspace system, the Secretary shall establish requirements for the safe operation of such aircraft systems in the national airspace system.

This section provided the FAA the opportunity to exempt certain types of aircraft from a more rigorous certification process and enable commercial operators to apply to use them in accordance with very specific operational considerations (U.S. Congress 2012). As these exemption applications began to come in by the thousands, the FAA released a "Blanket COA" that provided very basic restrictions that were beginning to seem like constant in the application process. Using the Wolf UAS LLC Exemption, #14873, and Certificate of Authorization (Blanket COA), the following common limitations are included:

- The aircraft could not be more than 55lb at time of flight including payload.
- Flights must be at or below 200ft AGL.
- VFR conditions only.
- Beyond five nautical miles from an airport with an operational tower.
- Three nautical miles from an airport having a published instrument flight procedure.
- Two nautical miles from an airport not having published instrument flight procedures.
- Two nautical miles from a heliport, gliderport, or seaplane base.
- The aircraft must be flown clear of, and give right of way to, manned aircraft.
- A visual observer, separate from the PIC, must be used at all times and maintain instantaneous communication.
- Remain clear of any Temporary Flight Restrictions (TFRs).
- Aircraft registration (identification) must be marked as largely as practicable.
- Documentation must be kept on site with operation at all times.
- A distant (D) Notice to Airman must be filed 24–48 hours prior to any commercial flight.
- Any accidents or incidents must be reported and the operator must file a monthly report on all flights that include locations, pilot names, UIAS

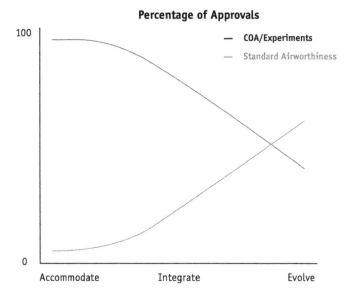

Figure 4.1 The FAA roadmap relationship between standard airworthiness and experimental or operationally approved flights

type and model, aircraft operational hours, and any failures, malfunctions, or damage (Department of Transportation 2015).

By coupling this operational approval with the exemption from airworthiness, the FAA essentially said that as long as you follow these operational mitigations, the risk to air safety is minimal when the aircraft is flown by an authorized pilot. Within the application process, it is stated that for the time being the FAA has not been granted the ability by Congress to remove, rescind, or reconsider the need for pilot certification as part of the Section 333 process. This, however, all changed when 14 CFR 107 was published on June 21, 2016. The Section 333 approval process changes dramatically with that publication as the vast need for operational approval for roughly 90 per cent of UAS use derives in the under-55lb category. What doesn't change is the need for operational approval for operations such as flight over people, BVLOS, night flying and those operations which are not covered under the new 14 CFR 107 regulations.

Major trends in drone regulatory developments continue. The first are the continuous regulatory developments that have come in the forms of state and local legislation and the other is the long wait for federally developed regulations. Some might say that both seem to be developed at the whim of lobbying groups intent on having their constituency's interest play the biggest role in their development. I would argue that regulation takes time to get right, and basing regulatory or legislative writings on the flippant frivolities of minor technology developments is not the way to go about it.

Two advances in federal regulation should be mentioned before moving on. One has already been touched upon, 14 CFR 107—the sUAS Rule—was published on June 21, 2016 and is the first APA-compliant regulatory development installed by August 21, 2016 (a mandatory 60-day waiting period exists for Final Rules). The other is a now specific push to develop operational approvals for specific types of operations including flight over people, beyond visual line of sight, or the micro category of UAS; 14 CFR 107 goes a long way in codifying much of what has already been discussed and therefore it may not be worth being redundant. What is important is that industry participants have the ability to fly commercial drone operations in safe environments, without a private or sports pilot license and without requiring the Section 333 Exemption Process for many operations. The 14 CFR 107 waiver applications for specific types of operations mostly replaced the Section 333 process. With the waiver process (found at www.faa.gov/uas/request_waiver), an applicant requests a waiver to fly: from a moving vehicle during night time, beyond the visual line of sight, without specific requirements regarding a visual observer, over people, in specific airspaces not allowed in 14 CFR 107, beyond 400 ft AGL, beyond the minimum visibility and distance from cloud requirements, without the need to yield right of way, and even operate multiple sUAS by one person.

The sUAS Final Rule, published June 21, 2016 contained much the same as the NPRM written and published in 2015[6] and contained basic operational requirements that would allow those described operations to not require special certification or exemption from 14 CFR aircraft airworthiness requirements. These requirements can be found in Table 4.3. While there are more operational requirements, readers are encouraged to look into this rule if they are interested in operating in the United States. The list in Table 4.3 is not comprehensive, but outlines the general requirements as set out in 14 CFR 107. As noted there are methods to go beyond these requirements, and continue to apply for airworthiness exemptions for any operations that are not covered in 14 CFR 107 as well as system design (most notably those larger than 55lb) to be used.

It is interesting to see that the maximum speed of these aircraft and the maximum altitude are actually much higher than in the blanket COAs or the proposed micro-UAS category to be discussed next. Also of note is that the FAA decreased the maximum flight altitude to 400ft AGL, from the originally proposed 500ft AGL limit.

Along those lines, the micro-UAS category that was proposed in the 14 CFR 107 NPRM is currently being discussed in two capacities. Most recently, the US Congress saw fit to include a micro-UAS amendment to the latest FAA Reauthorization Act entitled the Aviation Innovation, Reform & Authorization Act. Much like the FMRA of 2012, this act is what provides funding to the FAA for their operations, research, and overall mission success (US Congress 2016). While the House of Representatives passed the short-term extension for FAA reauthorization that included the micro-UAS category, the amendment was eventually rescinded (Power 2016). This category states that a drone could be used without ANY regulatory approval if it adheres to

Table 4.3 Summary of 14 CFR 107 Requirements for sUAS operations

Unmanned aircraft must weigh less than 55lbs	FPV flight does not satisfy sense and avoid Requirement
VLOS only	100mph maximum speed
No flights directly over non-participatory people	400ft AGL maximum altitude
CFR conditions only	No Class A operations
Yield right of way to other aircraft	ATC permission for B, C, D, E airspace operations
Preflight inspection required	Micro-UAS category proposed
VO not required but encouraged	One aircraft at a time for VO/PIC operation
Operators must pass an aeronautical knowledge test	Pass a knowledge test every 24 months
Operators must obtain a certification for sUAS	16 years or older to operate
Registration and aircraft marking required	Make the UA available for inspection by FAA
Report accidents within 10 days of any operation	Be vetted by TSA

flying below 400ft AGL, at an airspeed of no greater than 46mph, within visual line of sight, during daylight hours, and at least 5 miles from a tower-controlled airport unless they provide prior notice to the airport in question and receiver approval prior to the operation (R. Davis 2016). This amendment seems very reasonable, except that it was, unfortunately, being added at the very same time that the FAA is hosting an industry-based Aviation Rulemaking Committee (ARC) for precisely the same interest. Where Congress has already empowered the Federal Aviation Administration the ability to regulate drones safely, and the FAA is considered a much less politically motivated government institution than Congress, it is difficult to see the amendment as being in the interest of safety rather than in the interest of industry. While this political posturing and grapple between regulatory and legislative procedure is taking place, the unmanned aircraft community is also coming together through an APA-compliant method that provides a figurative estuary for discussion between regulators and industry in a standardized and collaborative way. This process is the standards development process and is considered one of the best ways for industry participants to shape the future of the technological evolution.

The Government Accountability Office also recognized the efforts of two non-governmental organizations in developing the Standards for Unmanned Aircraft Systems in the NAS. These two organizations, ASTM International Committee F-38 and RTCA SC-203 are both mentioned in the GAO report to Congress entitled, *Unmanned Aircraft Systems: Measuring Progress and Addressing Potential Privacy Concerns Would Facilitate Integration into the National Airspace System* (Government Accountability Office 2012).[7] RTCA Special Committee

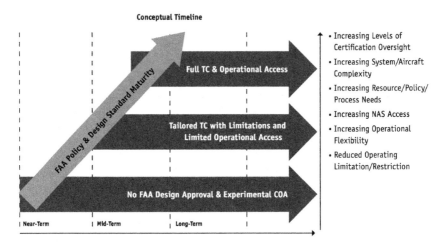

Figure 4.2 FAA envisioned relationship between standardization maturity and interim approval processes

is recognized as "a private, not-for-profit organization consisting of industry experts . . . Responsible for developing consensus-based recommendations and standards regarding UAS communications, navigation, surveillance, and air traffic management systems issues . . ." while ASTM F-38 is recognized as a "private organization consisting of industry experts that is responsible for developing standards and consensus based recommendations for small UAS integration into the national airspace system and worldwide" (Government Accountability Office 2012: 12).

The holy grail for integration of UAS is to create a fully fledged system of airworthiness certification that is flexible and responsive to advancing technologies and applications for UAS. It will not be enough to haphazardly determine operational approvals for medium or large UAS. The aviation environment requires deterministic, risk-based approaches to advancing operations through all risk categories. This is the pathway the FAA has laid out through the involvement of industry consensus standards, advisory committees, and processes that are no longer regulatory undefined. Figure 4.2 is taken from the FAA roadmap published in 2013.

Case study: The role of industry consensus groups – ASTM and RTCA

Working to develop the standards and practices for full integration into the national airspace are industry representatives, technical committees, academic institutions, and government representatives. RTCA SC-228 and ASTM F-38 serve similar roles for differing aircraft system categories—divided between the two based on size. Originally RTCA SC-203 was given the task of developing the standards and requirements necessary to safely integrate UAS into the NAS. Specifically, RTCA was asked to solve the problems related to the "limited human factors engineering incorporated into UAS technologies," "vulnerabilities in the command and control of UAS operations," and "the inability for UAS to detect, sense, and avoid other aircraft and airborne objects in a manner similar to 'see and avoid' by a pilot in a manned aircraft" (Walker 2010). The deliverables for RTCA SC-203 were to be "Minimum Aviation System Performance Standards" (MASPS) and "Minimum Operational Performance Standards" (MOPS); however RTCA SC-203 was sunset in 2013 and asked to discontinue its work in deference to a newly formed committee, RTCA SC-228. The reasons given were that SC-203 suffered from an attempt to "Boil the Ocean" by taking on too many challenges. However, having been on the committee and involved with leadership, what the committee lacked was an ability to decide upon prevailing system architecture in a manner satisfactory to executive leadership. All that to say, one company and their customers wanted air-based collision avoidance and communication architecture to be the standard for UAS while another company and their customer wanted ground-based radar to be the system of record for standards development.

Taking a break from the regulatory framework discussion for a moment, I want to share insight into the regulatory and standards process. Just as all the smaller manufacturers and operators hope to resolve issues and operate freely, the larger manufacturers—those that can spare the most manpower for this civic engagement—in turn get more say and are less inclined to promote a "freer" environment. Those larger manufacturers, in general, already encapsulate a large majority of the market share for research, innovation development, capital, government relationships, and in turn government contracts. What incentive is there for them to help ease the regulatory mire so that competition is increased? The mechanisms that have allowed these larger manufacturers to grow and perform have also defined these already successful company approaches and any change to the overall environment would also lead to a similar increase in competition.

I am not saying by any means that these companies are conspiring or colluding to prevent competition in the slightest. They are actively engaged in promoting the regulatory development of UAS integration into the NAS. However, I am saying that these companies have the largest say in the RTCA and ASTM committees by virtue of their ability to participate. These committees require membership fees as they are non-profit and unfunded by government. The time requirements in order to be actively engaged and involved are often more demanding than a small company, start-up, or even a mid-sized company can provide. As a result, the interests of smaller operators or manufacturers are often quieter than companies with a greater ability to participate. Representing academia as I have for the past six years of engagement, I have had the rare opportunity of having no agenda or product to push, and have therefore also been widely accepted into this process. I am not sure the same would be said for all commercial entities attempting to engage in the process, though as a technical chair for ASTM, I can say that the direct leadership promotes engagement of small business even when it is not demanded.

This has the direct result of reducing the incentive for quickening the pace by which regulation is created. Larger companies have more at risk for producing sub-par regulations with room to evolve rather than fully developed legal frameworks. Where the average operator on the street needs minimal instruction and guidance, the large companies want to be able to fly an unmanned Fed-Ex plane cross-country multiple times per night using the same framework. This again tends to demand all-encompassing regulation that works within the entirety of the well-established airspace, rather than special adjustments to low-altitude flight to accommodate the small operator.

What SC-228 has been tasked with after a leadership change has been to certify one type of UAS, within one environment. No longer is the regulatory framework being developed as system agnostic, or without reference to a system so as to be all-inclusive. Now the committee is focused on MASPS and MOPS for a focused UAS, within one environment, and for select mission profiles. Since this leadership change and new committee creation, much in the public environment has changed—putting pressure on the large UAS standard effort. However, RTCA is not developing the Small UAS standards which will generally be published first.

ASTM F-38 is the standards body tasked with developing the regulation for the Small Unmanned Aircraft Systems (sUAS). Comparatively, ASTM F-38 works in a much more diffuse and national way. While membership for RTCA is inclusive of many, the barriers to entry can be high. Time constraints, membership fees, and travel requirements for intimate involvement can dissuade otherwise interested parties from becoming participating and productive members. It can be expensive, time-consuming, and difficult to offer insight into the process. ASTM F-38, however, is much less expensive, often publishes their intentions on standards development, and is very active in social media. ASTM F-38 is tasked with developing those standards and requirements for the "small class" of UAS.

The FAA has not established or published a final categorization scheme for the certification criteria of UAS, and lobbying efforts have focused upon this pressure point recently. New lobbying groups and industry representatives see categorization of UAS as a method to gain access to airspace or be prevented from it.

We've got to know where we've been to know where we're going: An interview with Johnny Walker

When you ask anyone in unmanned aircraft, "Who are the leaders in the field of unmanned aircraft system integration," you'll get a variety of names. Some will identify those entrepreneurs who are leading Google's efforts in technology,

Amazon's battles with regulatory impediments, or journalists who have watched the field grow and develop for the last decade. There will always be one name, however, that pops up no matter whom you are talking to, and that person is Johnny Walker, co-founder of the Aerospace Consulting Company, The Padina Group. Johnny has a background in aviation that dwarfs all others who claim to be experts in the field of UAS and his insights into the direction of the industry come well rooted in its past. He's been there throughout the last 20 years of growth—from the smallest nod to the future of UAS integration to publication of 14 CFR 107, which is why we must appreciate it when he says, "We've got to know where we've been to know where we're going."

Johnny Walker credits his extensive career in unmanned aircraft systems to his years working within the FAA to create more advanced technological approaches to airspace. He spent 15 years in New York City with the FAA Eastern Region Air Traffic responsible for 7 states in the Northeast including Philadelphia, Washington, and the New York complex—all very busy traffic operations. In his last position, he served the country as the Air Traffic Division Manager. The real pathway into unmanned system integration efforts began, as he points out, "as he started doing some innovative airspace and air traffic management behavior focused on airports." This effort predated the latest NextGen efforts beginning in 1997. Within this involvement, FAA was doing things that were "ground breaking in looking at airspace design," technology promotion, and the degree to which equipage changes could be recommended or required. Johnny was asked to come to Washington as the Program Director of Airspace; to create a national airspace redesign that would outlay the next generation of airspace management for all aviation. Their task was to apply the legacy airspace system to a redesign that would allow for new technologies to develop and be applied. Johnny credits the key to that success, and eventually the foundation for UAS success, with the invitation of "stakeholders included everyone—airports, gliders, light aircraft, air carriers, air traffic, and others." Most importantly, though, he invited commercial space and unmanned aircraft to be a part of the conversation. Johnny recounts that, "1997 was the first time really the FAA brought in unmanned vehicles . . . We brought them into the planning because we knew they were important in the future of airspace." His foresight and ability to bring people together from a variety of industries would lay the foundation for success that has promoted UAS integration over the past two decades.

Johnny Walker's main focus has been in helping to lead the integration of UAS into the national airspace through the standards development process at RTCA. However, as Johnny points out, "it's important to understand where the RTCA efforts began." All the work began with a NASA initiative. In 2002 he got involved with the NASA Access 5 program—the first big program to integrate High Altitude Long Endurance (HALE) UAS into upper airspace over a five-year period. It was a $100 million NASA program that most people are not aware of. After only $30 million of the allocated budget was spent; the program was cancelled with renewed demand for NASA to go to Mars and the Moon. Prior to its cancellation, however, vital information had been gathered creating a cornerstone for UAS airspace integration and RTCA. As Johnny says, "That was the whole reason RTCA Special Committee-203 was even able to begin."

Before discussing Johnny's leadership at RTCA, it's vital to understand his development post-FAA and where his appreciation and knowledge for the complexities of sub-system integration continued. After leaving the FAA, Johnny Walker went on to work with a company called NAVERUS, purchased by GE, to develop Performance-Based Navigation (PBN). That time for him was very important for developing understanding and technology for the low-altitude airspace navigation work being done now by The Padina Group. He equates this low-altitude flight allowance to the

> railroads in the late 1800s. Vast areas are now open for flights, but no one knows how they will be run. The networks for UAS is very undefined in the two blocks of altitudes being allocated—low altitude and very high altitude. Will it be linear like the BNSF Railroad pathfinder at low altitude or not? The high altitude airspace above 60,000 feet will be highly complex, but we're just not sure how it will be managed yet and will require technological integration and understanding.

Since the current situation is evolving rapidly, the standards themselves will also iterate quickly.

Each opportunity, much like any new industry, led to another and coming out of his work at NAVERUS he began efforts with aerospace leaders of the UAS National Industry Team (UNITE). Through efforts at his consulting company The Padina Group, and his international contacts and relationships, he continued working with organizations that push the limits of UAS technologies, including support being done to help develop airworthiness certification for General Atomics Aeronautical Systems. Working with UNITE, through a program largely based on the ACCESS 5 and to help develop standards for UAS, Johnny began leading a variety of national and international efforts to develop standards for UAS. He also began efforts to coordinate activity and collaboration across international borders, as one of the largest issues with UAS is ensuring that the standards activities are not duplicating efforts and coming to different results. "In Aviation," Johnny points out:

> industry standards are well defined and closely aligned with bilateral agreements between many of the civil aviation authorities of states, including FAA, EASA, CASA, and NAV CANADA. Civil aviation organizations are aligned with ICAO in developing international Standards and Recommended Practices (SARPS). It is important that UAS, as just another part of aviation, develops the same way.

Clearly, Johnny Walker and his team at the FAA were right about the need to include UAS integration in the future of airspace, and nearly two decades after he began to build those relationships, we've seen the approach flourish. What started as a simple invitation to industry leaders has become an ecosystem of cross-collaboration, cooperation, and coopetition. While the development of UAS regulations and standards seems inevitable now, it wasn't until 2006 when the first FAA UAS policy memo was published and another ten years before the sUAS Final Rule would be published.

So, where are we now? Well, when asked about where standards groups are going and how the RTCA, ASTM, EUROCAE, or ISO deliverables will be used with the technology of drones moving so rapidly, Mr. Walker had an intriguing answer. "This is a new form of aviation, and UAS needs to look, smell, and breathe like the rest of aviation," he replies, "The business case will be large metropolitan areas" and eventually those unique challenges will be addressed. He goes on:

> When standards efforts were started no one was thinking of the standards for things like sense-and-avoid, 14 CFR 91.1.13. When you're looking at the regulations it doesn't matter if you're at 60,000ft or 900ft. Those are very different airspaces and using technology that aid you in one while not in the other. At high altitudes it's very unlikely that an airplane will willy-nilly come near you that you need to avoid. The airspace is highly regulated, but at lower altitudes or less controlled airspace you have other issues. UAS will still have to respond to these odd challenges that even manned aviation can have trouble dealing with.

He's right: a great debate still rages as to the requirement for adopting TCAS or ADS-B in the NextGen initiatives.

Johnny says that in his time leading RTCA SC 203, and his involvement throughout the world's various standards efforts, they have had to address these integration issues that will need to evolve alongside manned aviation equipage requirements. In the beginning at RTCA SC-203, they "spent 18 months trying to determine the scope of what was required to integrate UAS into the airspace. It was all the people involved at RTCA who had to try to put rigor into what was being required for UAS operations." When SC-203 was ended and SC-228 created in recent years, "some people said RTCA 203 was trying to boil the ocean, but much of the work required scoping of the project from the ground up." It is no wonder, then, that SC-203 had a hard time coming to meaningful conclusions when the very understanding of UAS operations and systems had to be scoped from the very beginning.

These discussions and industry group reports are still important, even if no deliverables have been created that establish a standard for the industry. Much of the work by Johnny's teams, and the author of this book, still goes on in use relating to human factors system description, communications and control elements, and CONOPS descriptions. Johnny appreciates this environment for collaboration, and he outlines the process to illustrate the way these discussions become impact:

When industry recommendations are formed, and FAA are sitting in the room, the discussion swirls back and forth and the product goes to a final resolution. All of the comments have to be adjudicated. You finally come to a product, it becomes a DO (DOcument) and goes to the FAA. The FAA still has the right to accept all, some, or none of the recommendations. It is rare that the FAA doesn't adopt the recommendations and put into FARs or orders, or Advisory Circulars.

In other words, the impact may not be immediate, but it drives the way regulations are interpreted, enforced, or adhered to.

What can be troubling in this process is duplicating efforts and coming to conclusions that differ across borders. When differences arise, some may look at efforts that took years and become disheartened, but Johnny Walker sees it as a time to rise up, reach out, and establish new relationships to fix the problem. When "you had this issue" he begins,

> with all other standards organizations for other industries and you have other work going, you reach problematic solutions. An example is something as simple as electrical plugs . . . you can create a system that doesn't make sense. Aviation is different; it is all standardized across the industry so you don't need an adapter. Aviation standards have got to be global and you need to work together to ensure that happens . . . EUROCAE Work Group 73 was born out of this need for cross-collaboration between the standards groups. The work wouldn't be identical, but there would be a similar approach that would match on both sides of the Atlantic. EUROCAE products go to EASA. EASA and the FAA have bilateral agreements, so the work really needed to be synergistic.

By helping to develop this unique collaborative methodology, not officially but with presentations to one another, the efforts across oceans would continue in a proactive and meaningful way.

With regard to standards groups in the United States, Johnny also makes it a point to identify the work done at ASTM and led by Ted Wierzbanowski as having a fundamental role in sUAS development. "It's important to mention ASTM," he reminds us,

> ASTM has a long story for reason of being involved in sUAS. When AUVSI was led by Daryl Davis as Executive Director, we were looking for the FAA—in 2002 or 2003-time frame - to work in an industry government relationship. There was not an umbrella yet to do that, there could have been, but the FAA chose not to do it.

While the UAS relationship had not yet been established in ASTM,

> the Light sport rule came out of ASTM in conjunction with, and in formal relationship with the FAA. There were one or two folks from AUVSI

that came to ASTM to do an activity with UAS, which is how F38 got started. Jim Williams (Former UAS Program Lead) came on board 5 years later or so, and saw the value from ASTM, and Ted Wierzbanowski came on board and helped lead ASTM efforts.

This would be a very important shift within ASTM and the FAA relationship in which ASTM and FAA, led by Wierzbanowski and Williams respectively, could work in an official capacity to design sUAS standards for the industry. While there is no official relationship between RTCA or ASTM "many of the same members operate within both."

These standards groups have been working collaboratively with government entities, industry partners, and stakeholders, then, for 20 years or more and Johnny Walker has been at the center of all of it. His unique insight into the direction of the international standards environment is one that cannot be challenged. So, when asked about the future of UAS work internationally, his optimism should be believed. In 2003 the accepted global view was that commercial UAS would be years and years away from becoming a reality. At that time Doug Davis was leading FAA activities, and an informal meeting was held at ICAO which issued a state letter to 139 states; and the response from that letter was overwhelmingly "Yes we want a UAS study group." The study group rapidly became the RPAS panel, which in ICAO talk was galactic in speed, which is unprecedented. The next steps forward must be international, which is why he has begun working across the globe. It began humbly, when a joint meeting in Palm Coast, Florida in January 2007, between FAA, ICAO, RTCA, EUROCAE ICAO, agreed "that ICAO should coordinate the development of a strategic guidance document that would guide the regulatory evolution" of UAS. (Note: this is taken from the ICAO AC328 Document, page 1 that cites the Palm Coast Meeting.)

This international effort continues, and Johnny is involved in the creation of a new UAS committee ISO/TC 20/SC16 Unmanned Aircraft Systems. As chairman of this new committee, Johnny is ensuring that no duplicative efforts will be made with RTCA, ASTM, SAE, or EUROCAE. As Johnny puts it,

> RTCA is primarily for Americans, EUROCAE is for Europeans, ASTM also Americans, China has CAPE, Singapore has SONG. ISO will be 18 states that includes participation from across the globe and looks at the safety and quality piece that ISO is known for. Meanwhile, the Joint Authorities for Rulemaking on Unmanned Systems (JARUS) has taken on a life of its own and also leads global activities with UAS work groups.

He sees the FAA's role in all of these standards organizations continuing under Earl Lawrence's leadership within the UAS Program Office as well, and believes the FAA "will continue to work with all standards groups and international organizations to identify UAS requirements. We have a delicious opportunity to continue both formal and informal conversations just to talk through things" with the expanded goal of influencing positive support for international UAS standards development.

While these standards groups continue their work, Johnny also outlines how ICAO fits prominently into the whole global system. "Most of the technical information driving ICAO recommendations" Johnny asserts,

> are coming from the states participating in ICAO development. Transport Canada and Nav Canada play a very key role in all of this. When the folks come in from Europe you have the major players. You get America, South Africa, Brazil, and a strong delegation from the Pacific Rim including Japan, China, South Korea, Singapore, Australia and New Zealand. There are many bilateral agreements for airspace management throughout the world that all must be considered at the ICAO level for developing SARPs.

Finally, Johnny Walker addressed what he believes the greatest catalyst for driving industry forward will be, and his answer was fascinating and directly relevant to this book. "Once we adopt, internationally" he begins,

> a risk-based approach, as far as what that risk is to that operation, and what that volume of airspace is, that is huge. A linear operation along a railroad track then becomes possible as it is differentiated from populated people. Something in an unpopulated area has a different risk profile that now becomes possible. Equipage changes, business cases are now made possible. Risk characteristics will be the number one thing to get our arms wrapped around for acceptance.

A risk-based approach is the core of the movement within the FAA and internationally, and is directly the reason for incorporating lessons learned in a Safety Management System (SMS). "Look what is happening," he continues,

> we have tremendous breakthroughs in technology that are helping to discover solutions for what is sense and avoid. Airborne sense and avoid, like that developed by General Atomics, is something tangible beyond just something you have on paper. This integration into NAS projects have something to work with and it will be important for what FAA ties into approvals.

Johnny Walker is a true leader in the field of unmanned aircraft systems in the purest sense. He leads from the front, being involved through standards and in the application of drones all over the world. The most important takeaway in speaking with him is that stakeholders must be involved from the beginning; the more the better. While technology will adapt, the people involved in the process provide the foundation for reasonable forward-thinking standards that will enable the industry to flourish and adapt.

5 Concept of Operations: One size does not fit all

Everything we do in life must begin with a plan, whether that plan is thought out through discussion or dialogue, written out on paper, outlined via regulations and standard operating procedures, or well-defined and purposefully ingrained habits that transcend active decision processing. Those habits may not seem purposeful, but the reason you know that part of the plan to brush your teeth is that as a child, you developed that habit through constant reinforcement. That reinforcement created a Standard Operating Procedure (SOP) before bed, and now it's assumed that you'll brush your teeth before bed. It doesn't have to be written, and everyone is on the same page.

Flying is similar. To create positive habits, develop those SOPs, and get everyone on the same page, you must begin with clear and distinct direction that is reinforced and promoted without fail. However, before those SOPS can be created and before clear understanding of how to approach a mission exists, all personnel involved must have a clear understanding of the overall system and operation. People make poor decisions without clear boundaries or knowledge of what they are making decisions about. If I don't know the possible weather scenarios for a particular area or the wind tolerances for my aircraft, how can I decide when a mission should be a "go or no go" and how do I decide when to use a different aircraft?

It is important to understand as much as possible about the overall mission and what complexities exist prior to flight. This activity of willful and directed understanding in aviation is often recognized as the most important element of any flight: mission planning, system knowledge, personnel briefing, and contingency awareness all rely on mutual understanding of the various factors that can, and will, impact flight. By taking the initial step to understand as much as possible about a mission, the crew members gain insight into how their actions or inactions drive the outcomes for mission success. This process takes practice and must be repeated; however, the time and energy spent in fleshing out each mission will save resources, materials, and possibly even lives, down the road. This process of initial understanding and outlining of specific characteristics is often called the Concept of Operations (CONOPS), and this chapter is dedicated to understanding what is entailed in a successful CONOPS as well as why these elements are incorporated. The last section of this chapter illustrates how various industries will find the process helpful, and provides comparative differences to show how "one size does not fit all" when it comes to UAS operations.

The Concept of Operations (CONOPS) can have many definitions and be outlined in a variety of ways depending on the type of organization or mission taking place. The level of attention given to the CONOPS likewise impacts the effectiveness of the activity. The old adage, "you get out what you put in," is extremely relevant here though the need for highly complex CONOPS documentation and awareness may be less important in less complex systems or for missions with fewer risk associations as defined by the Operational Risk Assessment process discussed later in the book.

Not only does a CONOPS affect the overall success of a mission, and provide better understanding of the mission and system, but it is also required by the FAA, and most international CAAs, for approvals to fly in national airspace. While regulations throughout the world change monthly, a requirement to understand the overall Concept of Operations will not change. Further, the more thorough and thoughtful a CONOPS is, the more likely it is to be accepted by the relevant aviation authority. It is imperative that those seeking approvals or certifications beyond the most minimal classifications of UAS activity (mini in the United States or open in Europe) understand the required elements of a well-developed CONOPS, how to document that CONOPS, and what the effects are on their efforts.

The question remains, what is a CONOPS? Well, for that we look to MITRE™ for one of the best definitions available for a CONOPS. MITRE™ defines a CONOPS as:

> A user-oriented document that describes systems characteristics for a proposed system from a user's perspective. A CONOPS also describes the user organization, mission, and objectives from an integrated systems point of view and is used to communicate overall quantitative and qualitative system characteristics to stakeholders.
>
> (MITRE 2016)

They look at a CONOPS as a way for "operational needs, desires, visions, and expectations of the user" to be outlined and defined so that all involved in a mission can be on the same page. By enhancing communications and allowing stakeholders involved throughout the mission—executives, managers, operators/pilots, visual observers, clients, manufacturers, etc.—the CONOPS minimizes the possibility of miscommunication, provides an accessible location for assumptions and priorities, and outlines the very basic foundations of the mission. This minimizes the "silo effect" of communication, promotes inter-stakeholder understanding, and provides the necessary foundation for mission development.

While the development of communication across parties is a fundamental purpose of the CONOPS, another important factor is that hazard identification

Figure 5.1 Core elements of the safety case for use in approvals by
FAA and/or other CAAs

and risk analysis cannot take place without a clear understanding of the mission, system, personnel, and contingency planning. The CONOPS allows better evaluation for safety of the operation through the Operational Risk Assessment (ORA) Process and the larger Safety Management System development. For operations over people, beyond visual line of sight, extended line of sight, close to airports, in-doors and anything beyond very basic limitations as set by CAAs, these processes are all recognized as necessary elements of the overall safety case and therefore should be understood to exist together as shown in Figure 5.1.

All four elements—SMS, CONOPS, ORA, and Risk Mitigations—work to describe a safety-focused, mission-driven, adaptive, and reasonable approach to unmanned flight that is both legal and safe. Let's turn now to what is entailed in a CONOPS and why the characteristics of that CONOPS drive mission success and act as an integral part of the safety development process. It also is important to note that the CONOPS should be undertaken many times as the system or environment changes. As the system, environment, personnel, training, or any other element changes so too do the assumptions, perceptions, and knowledge of the system.

Elements of a Concept of Operations

System description

System design may seem like an element of the CONOPS that should be taken care of and out of the way before missions and operations take place, and for many operators this is true. Most commercial operators, and all hobbyist operators today, have very little control on the parts and designs that define their system. They have little authority over the control mechanisms when flying an out-of-the-box solution. Manufacturers have already decided what C2 link exists, how that will function in times of low or non-GPS connectivity, wireless interference, and directional communications loss. However, the need to understand the system and components, as well as how they fail, has not diminished. So it is important to break down the different parts of the system into manageable, definable, and often controllable sub-portions. According to the Standard Practice for Operational Risk Assessment of Small Unmanned Aircraft Systems (sUAS) F3178-16 from ASTM F-38, "The primary elements of a SUAS are . . . the aircraft, control station, crew, and control link and data/telemetry communications link parameters" (ASTM F-38.02 Work Group 2016).

Aircraft:

- A description of the aircraft should include limitations of the aircraft. What is the maximum bank angle or speed tolerance? How high is the airframe capable of flying and for how long? What limits this maneuverability—battery life, aerodynamics, payload, weight and balance, etc.?
- Normal procedures.
- Emergency procedures.
- Supplemental Information and systems information for any aircraft intended for operation.
- Sub-systems that have direct impact on the safety of flight: flight guidance, powerplant, fuel and batteries, propellers or rotors, electrical systems and equipment, and radio and navigation equipment not already addressed should be included.

Control station:

- A description of the structure, occupancy limitations, components, mobility, and weather tolerances should be included for the control elements of the aircraft.
- How does the control station meet any regulatory requirements? Does it require a pilot and visual observer (VO) for mission allowance and success? Will the pilot be flying in first- or third-person visual?

Crew members:

- A clear and concise description of the qualifications and training for the PIC, VO, any other crew member, and management access to those individuals throughout the flight.
- Outline the responsibilities of each crew member for pre-flight, flight, and post-flight conditions.

Command and control (C2) link:

- A description of the power and frequency for the operation of the aircraft, susceptibility to compromise of the C2 link.
- Strategies for preventing deliberate and non-deliberate compromise of those systems.
- The range of operation based on C2 capabilities.

Data/telemetry communications link:

- A description of the data and telemetry being gathered.
- Strategies for maintaining safe operation and storage of data and communications.
- Regulatory requirements if necessary for control of data.

Operational description

Operational design is where most of the control exists for proponents and operators of a sUAS mission and where most of the risk in unmanned aviation is being addressed currently by civil aviation authorities. Without delving too much into the domestic and international regulatory environments, as they are addressed in depth in other chapters, we can say that operational risk mitigation is the method by which approval processes are moving forward fastest. The Section 333 Exemption Process in the United States, reliant upon the Certificate of Authorization or Waiver (COA) and the new 14 CFR 107 Waiver application process, looks at where the operation is taking place, what the purpose of that mission is, and how to prevent risk to those in the air and on the ground in the likelihood of a crash. These COAs limit the location, altitude, speed, proximity to infrastructure and crowds, and a number of other operationally focused elements that minimize risk operationally.

The portion of the CONOPS that deals with operations is likewise the most likely place that will allow applicants to minimize risk convincingly and thereby gain access to the national airspace. The following elements are taken from FAA guidance, discussions with FAA Airframe Certification Office, Small Airplane Directorate, and from the ASTM F-38.02 Standards. As operational considerations are vital to any type of operation, these same elements can be applied to manned aviation, underwater unmanned systems, and ground operations. They exist to create a thorough, precise, and well-communicated understanding of a mental model for operations. These may not all be applicable to your operation. It is important to remember that this CONOPS is developed to provide the necessary elements for all types of applicants in the UAS environment for approval—including higher-risk missions over people, beyond line of sight, and in urban environments with full automation.

Overall operation:

- Offer a description of all operational scenarios for the sUAS for visual line of sight (VLOS), beyond line of sight (BVLOS), and extended line of sight (EVLOS) operations.
- Include a brief description of the types of operations that are planned:
  - Outline the specific use—agricultural multispectral imaging or spraying, power-line inspections or transformer inspections, industrial inspection, film or TV videography or cinematography, etc.

- Describe the nature of the company's business. Are you a manufacturer, operator, system integrator, tester, educator, etc.?
  - This has relevance for the "public interest" element of the evaluative process that addresses tolerable risk by the public versus need of your operation.
- Describe and define the geographical operating boundary:
  - The less specific you are, the more access you are requesting. This could result in an initial refusal of your mission approval process.
- Describe and define any intent to launch/fly/recover only over private or public property.
  - Private property requests limit your access to NAS and thereby increase the likelihood of your approval. However, it also limits your access to the NAS to a degree that may prevent you from accomplishing your goal.
- Define the minimum and maximum operating characteristics:
  - These should include regulatory limitations accordingly to your approvals federal or municipal regulations.
  - These should also include aircraft characteristic limitations or company limitations that exist in the interest of safety.
- Include the ability, regulatory approval for, and intentions, to operate within or beyond visual line of sight (BVLOS) and/or EVLOS.
- Describe the populations that exist within the proposed operating area:
  - This should include those in the air and on the ground. Remember qualitative descriptions are fine for these evaluations so long as they are based on factual information or based on experience of a subject matter expert.
- Understand, describe, and explain the airspace classes of the operating area.
- Describe the location of the control station:
  - Identify if the control station will be moving, who has access to the control station, where V/O will be stationed in relation to the CS, and if the PIC will be in, around, or near the CS area at all time.
  - Automation may not require a constant PIC interaction for long flights; however it is crucial to understand where the PIC will be and what ongoing responsibilities are in relation to physical contact with the CS.

Summary of sUAS operations for all users in the area—including those in the air and on the ground:

- Identify any special considerations, postings, or communications needed in the type of airspace being flown within:
  - Understand that Class E Airspace has different characteristics and that one flight environment is never the same as the next. Hospitals, schools, power-lines and utilities, public sensitivities, and even private property all may require different actions and communications on the

part of the operator and it is very important to address these concerns ahead of time.

- Clearly define and outline the launch and recovery details, locations, and personnel:
  – Outline methods used if necessary, and explain any significant notices for crew members that may be unusual or usual.
- Identify and discuss the operation's proximity to people, infrastructure, structures, vehicles, prohibited areas, or restricted areas and how to identify them from the ground or air:
  – Discuss the impact of flight beyond boundaries that may occur and how to mitigate the risk of damage to sensitive locations.
- Identify and discuss the potential for proximity to other airspace users and the tolerance for incursion into another's airspace.
- Coordinate and develop procedures for understanding the meteorological conditions in which the operation will take place, what the tolerances for weather (visual/instrument conditions, icing, wind gusts) are for the airframe or control station:
  – Often, air vehicles will be the limiting factor when it comes to weather as icing becomes a significant problem, internal electronics freeze or batteries become less efficient. It is important to note that these will affect an operation and therefore advanced knowledge and contingency planning based on weather changes are a vital portion of the CONOPS.
- Identify and define the automation levels of the operation and the capabilities of the airframe in all events:
  – Will the aircraft be flown using autopilot, manual control, stabilization assistance beyond what is an industry standard?
  – Is there a return to home condition or loiter/hold position condition that will be used? How does the return to home function work? Does it return directly or can it avoid obstacles if they are sensed in their pathway?
  – Will the flight plan be uploaded to the aircraft or does it have the ability to be taken over mid-flight by controller in the event of mission change?
  – Automation is a very significant portion that must be well understood by all crew members and significant time should be taken during this section.
- Coordinate and define minimum crew for the organization fly and what the roles of those crew members must be.
- Discuss any intent to fly over people that are not involved directly in the operation planning:
  – Have they been notified? Have you posted signage letting them know that aerial footage is being done in the area?
  – As privacy is the most significant concern to much of the public, understanding that communicating with people you will be flying near

or over is one of the best ways to mitigate your risk of exposure and law suit (Walls 2014).

- Identify the pilot to aircraft ratio (1:1 etc.):
  - As swarm aircraft technologies develop, and PIC are allowed to pursue multiple aircraft to one pilot, this will become a sticking point for applicants and operators alike.
- Determine and record whether operations will take place at night or whether all will be taken during the day.
- Define the plan for crew member physical and mental safety:
  - Have you incorporated any fatigue management programs?
  - Are there limitations to on-sight exposure to volatile chemicals and weather?
  - Are there first-aid kits and have crew members been trained in first-aid and CPR?
- Describe the training level of each crew member directly related to the operation being discussed in concrete terms:
  - This is a follow-up to earlier training requirements and directly affects those chosen for the mission.
  - This portion comes up in the Operational Risk Assessment as deficiencies in training and certification may include any physical, mental, or operational issues that will affect mission success and safety.
- Delineate any community outreach plans that will be used to minimize risk to those on the ground or in the air:
  - Community outreach may include signage near the flight environment, Notices to Airmen (NOTAMs), operational awareness information that has been distributed to airports, ATC, municipal community meetings, etc.
  - The more engaged you are with the community, the more accepting they will be in doing their part to minimize risk.
- Describe when, how, or if flight plans will be filed with air traffic control.
- Identify the crew member responsible to act as the central point of contact with the local ATC and other community members.
- Describe the applicable accident or incident reporting procedures, and when, in what form, and where the reports can be located.

Outline command, control, and communications functions as well ATC or traffic management conditions:

- Detail plans involving the command and communications functions between the different components of the sUAS and NAS stakeholders:
  - This gets to the question of onboard ADS-B, sense-and-avoid (SAA) technologies, separation through ATC coordination, and other technology elements that may be utilized for segregating airspace.
- Describe any command and communication functions between the sUAS components and sub-systems to include the aircraft, control station, control link, observers, etc.:

- – Can a V/O take over command of the plane? Is there a sensor operator with the ability to take over control? Is the aircraft equipped with a TCAS that can override user input?
- – Is there geo-fencing technology enabled that will disallow inputs for flight into terrain, buildings, or geo-tagged airspace?
- Outline any security parameters or conditioning for the C2 link:
  - – Is your C2 link protected from interference or hacking?
- Describe the methods by which situational awareness will be maintained at all times:
  - – If the public tries to speak with you do you have someone with you to handle that interaction?
  - – Is there a procedure in place while flying to prevent accident and engage with on-site interference be it individual, animal, system, or environmental condition?

The following elements are directly related to larger UAS operating in the NAS in Class A airspace, in more complex and high-risk environments, or with more complex system engineering-based reliability. While small UAS can absolutely benefit from incorporating these elements into their CONOPS, they are focused for an applicant looking to operate BVLOS, in direct coordination with ATC using instrument flight rules, and utilizing longer flight time.

- Describe the number of pilots that will be used throughout the mission lifecycle as well as hand-off procedures between individuals and control stations as they apply.
- Define the PIC at all times throughout the operation including through hand-offs for record keeping and decision-making at strict mission intervals.
- Describe and outline the lost-link procedures for loss or interruption of positive control as well as contingency planning for extended lost-link procedures:
  - – Will the aircraft return to home on its own? Will it continue to fly the mission without control input?
  - – This is a critical element of flight planning stage and must be well understood prior to the ORA activity.
- Define any communication protocols, procedures, and expectations with air traffic control.
- Define emergency procedures and include a copy of the emergency response plan for immediate access and ensure harmonization between definition.

By going through this process and understanding the value of the Concept of Operations activity, all members of the crew as well as the civil aviation authority that oversees the national airspace coordination and safety will be speaking the same "safety language." The industry must undertake these types

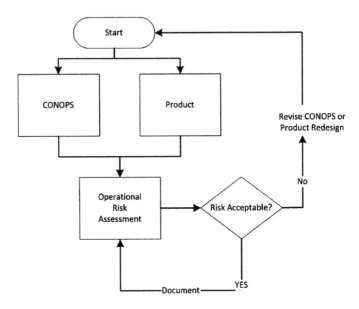

Figure 5.2 The Concept of Operations (CONOPS) lifecycle diagram

of activities until the systems are reliable in nature, the environment is readily accessible, and the risk tolerance by the public is much higher. Even then, the CONOPS activity and documentation is an extremely worthwhile modality for understanding the very components that define a UAS operation and one that should be taken very seriously. The CONOPS ORA Relationship Flowchart outlines how the CONOPS interfaces with a risk assessment activity—acting as a systems level method for identifying potential hazards, providing a foundation to mitigate those risks, and then cyclically evolve with that analysis.

The CONOPS flowchart shows a generic process for addressing a new mission or use for UAS and the need to understand what system, product in this flowchart, and mission parameters to use. The flowchart shows how the CONOPS remains often separate because this activity is for users of the system (operators) rather than for manufacturers. As the needs that will define the system evolve and are identified, and the system design is well understood, the Operational Risk Assessment takes both and addresses the identified hazards for their risk score (this process is outlined later in the book). If the risks are deemed acceptable the CONOPS and ORA can be documented and the flight move forward. If the risks are deemed unacceptable, an organization can go back to redefine the CONOPS, address system shortcomings in the UAS itself, or address the risks differently.

Case study: One size does not fit all

The most important use for a CONOPs is of course the need to understand as much as possible about you, your business, your drone, and your mission before getting into a risky environment or putting institutional resources at risk. The tendency for individuals is to believe that "one size fits all" when it comes to drones, and the consumer markets have spent a significant amount of money in developing that notion in consumers. This is assuredly a symptom of the way investment works as investors need their money to make the biggest investment in large markets. If the consumer product they are investing in does not address a substantially sized market segment, they are less interested and the funding streams dry up. The drone companies in turn promote themselves as being a great solution to as many problems as possible. All of a sudden they can carry a payload or sensor with optimal efficiency for all applications—agriculture, law enforcement, inspections, real estate, photogrammetry—the works.

The following case study sections illustrate how a CONOPs can help those in different industries understand their differences, design a better system or operation through the rigorous CONOPs protocol, and follow compliance with major civil aviation authority requirements.

I've learned quite a bit from teaching and one of the techniques I find most valuable is case study analysis. Over the next few sections we'll look at different industries through the eyes of a CONOPs. We'll begin to look at what an end-user may not understand for different industries that are ripe for drone use, yet untapped in complexity. These industries will likely be in the news for drone enthusiasts, but may not be on the forefront of the tech-space community, or relatively unknown in the industries themselves. Sure, everyone in the drone community world knows that wind-turbine inspections are taking place all over the world by using innovative UAS companies, but many utility companies are unaware of the intricacies, evolving technologies, or even required support services for that application.

First response and crisis management

First responders to natural disasters, industrial catastrophes, law enforcement actions, revolutions, and even transportation accidents are finding value through the use of unmanned aircraft, ground and underwater vehicles. DARPA has spent millions on the need for robotics through their DARPA robotics challenge leading to innovations in the hardware, software, and sensor platforms requisite for efficient and effective use. The lessons learned from these challenges, from use cases all over the world, and industry needs are not being taken into consideration for the design of these advanced systems for large companies. Simply put, off-the-shelf hardware is not sufficient for ensuring continued use in diverse conditions, weather conditions that limit use due to humidity or wind, and infrastructure that can be detrimental to performance.

Crisis response needs robust and hardened solutions—not consumer-grade products that are unreliable even in the best conditions. They don't need uncontrolled flyaway due to incompatible Wi-Fi connections, they need safe and secure C2 links and ruggedized sensor platforms.

First responders have certain requirements when it comes to their mission that all go to defining the most important element for drone use—the Concept of Operations or CONOPS. The CONOPS includes the most vital considerations for drone system design and operation. These considerations are also all required for operational certification and approval by civil aviation authorities and therefore it simply makes sense to address the needs ahead of time, before investing in hardware/software. These include:

1. *Type of operation—Visual line of sight, extended line of sight, or beyond line of sight*: For crisis management or first response, say in the case of an earthquake that has devastated the country side, line of sight and extended line of sight may be all that is required. This simplifies and directly impacts the type of communication links you need and the approval process by the state is much simpler.
   a. First responders may need access to extended line of sight or beyond line of sight characteristics as their mission may include combining census data with topographical scans of damage to those in remote locations. By combining these two outlets of information instantly, operators can locate the most endangered populations—the elderly at home, hospitals, and schools—with the most damage to do the most good.
2. *Definition of flight area and airspace—Population density, expected air traffic, expected surface traffic, types of buildings or vital infrastructure in the area, any confined or obstructed areas, emergency landing areas or terminal flight areas*: Understanding these items makes planning flight time needs, sense-and-avoid technologies, and payload weights much easier and allows for a clear understanding of the system design with regard to battery size, motor control and size, and communications needs including GPS, directional links, etc.
3. *Conditions for operations—Wind speed limitations (headwind, crosswind, gust), turbulence restrictions, minimum visibility conditions, outside air temperature limits*: Fundamentally one of the least considered sections when preparing for crisis management. Applicants often find themselves with 75 per cent on-site downtime due to inclement weather and a lack of preparation or planning for purchasing systems that can handle various weathers. There is a reason Aerovironment's PUMA AE™ is expensive—it can allow mission successful in difficult environments where the other fixed-wings, unintended for those environments, cannot.
4. *Payloads or sensor needs—Configurations, usability, lighting conditions, proximity to scanning environment, clarity and resolution needs, timeline for access to data, data security and management*: First responders to accidents, fires, or radioactive conditions may require data much quicker than those who are

simply monitoring damage or assessing infrastructure cost estimates. The system should not remain the same, and likewise the hardware/software being used is not the same. The needs of firefighters in active conditions are not the same as a surveyor sent to monitor the site-conditions of a damaged church. Some payloads are modular, others are not.

5. *UAS performance characteristics—Maximum altitude (not regulatory), maximum airspeed, cruise or hover airspeed, maximum endurance, maximum range, maximum rate of climb/descent, maximum bank angle, turn rate limits, payload capacity, battery draw*: Notice that these come last, as all elements to be considered should DRIVE the characteristic requirements of the UAS. If you find that the drone you have selected is not directly related to the mission requirements, it is time to find a new system.

First response is different for every organization—Team Rubicon™ approaches it differently from the Red Cross™. It is critical that the mission drives the system requirements. Whether you're flying in Nepal to assess earthquakes at 350ft AGL in light weather conditions or flying near extensive and sensitive infrastructure in high-wind events using micro-uav systems, your requirements will be different and you must consider the design and operations from the very beginning.

Drones for inspections

This is the second post in the CONOPs case study and one that will shine some light on the way that the energy sector is approaching UAS inspections. The energy sector for the purposes of this includes oil and gas, solar, and electrical grid power-lines, though wind-power, nuclear power, and tidal/geothermal power are also looking into using UAS for different needs including surveillance, monitoring, and maintenance inspections.

There are significant success stories throughout the UAS community high-lighting inspections, and for good reason. While generally less "autonomous" in nature, the hardware and profile of a drone operation allows users to diminish the significant risk to the operation. Perhaps the most interesting element of these market segments is that each approaches the solution in a different way. The greatest success stories from the oil and gas sector seem to center on "drones as a service," where oil platform management (Shell, ConocoPhillips, Chevron, etc.) engage with companies such as Cyberhawk™ or Aeryon Labs™ to inspect flare stacks for corrosion, heat damage, and other degradation that may harm the overall system. Meanwhile, the solar and wind energy industry has seen that both fixed-wing aircraft and rotorcraft (hexacopters and octocopters) can be assets to their operations, though generally the consensus seems to be settling on VTOL aircraft with a hexa or octo configuration. Lastly, power-line maintenance and inspection are rapidly deploying UAS for both inaccessible environments and long-distance higher-altitude monitoring, experimenting with both VTOL and fixed-wing UAS.

While mixed approaches ultimately benefit the industry as experience and understanding develop, corporate entrepreneurs seeking to implement cost-saving, safety-increasing, efficiency-promoting UAS don't have the time, energy, or corporate buy-in to squander. That's where the initial system development and understanding come into play. Corporate entrepreneurs that fall prey to slick sales people selling off-the-shelf products or services in a "one size fits all" approach will find their future work more difficult or impossible. The demands and needs of each type of organization differ. This is where the Concept of Operations phase of any development process begins and why it is so vital to ensuring success for your organization.

The basic elements of any CONOPS include the following elements, discussed within the context of inspections:

1. Type of operation—Visual line of sight, extended line of sight, or beyond line of sight:
   a. *Oil and gas inspections*—While the regulatory situation in the United States is not clearly defining the timeline for BLOS and ELOS operations, it is clear the oil and gas inspections—when it comes to some operations (flare stack inspections, vertically focused inspections, and centrally located silos or perimeter maintenance)—focus generally on direct line of sight capabilities. This is a main reason for the success of drone use in this field as VLOS operation demand does not negate the usefulness of the operation.
   b. *Solar energy farms*—VLOS is generally fine for direct inspection of infrastructure though we have witnessed need for extended line of sight frequently as hills between solar arrays often require movement of GCS location and deployment. This increases time, in situ movement requirements, and leads to more flights.
   c. *Power-line inspection*—Power-line inspection will become viable and extremely important when beyond line of sight operations become frequent. Two types of operations currently exist in the power-line inspection market—vertical examination of the structure and trans-former condition and horizontal examination across grid sections using LiDAR and photogrammetric appraisal. The sensor load and need ultimately drives the mission requirements in this field, and therefore BLOS and ELOS will be necessary in some, but not all, cases.
2. Definition of flight area and airspace—Population density, expected air traffic, expected surface traffic, types of buildings or vital infrastructure in the area, any confined or obstructed areas, emergency landing areas or terminal flight areas:
   a. *Oil and gas inspections*—Often these operations take place over water, in high safety requirement zones. Sensitive Infrastructure exists and therefore designs that are robust and rugged with avionics that may be able to avoid collision (as seen in the latest DJI videos) may be a

necessity when wind gusts arise or conditions change. A crash is not tolerable in these conditions other than to ditch into water, though the oil and gas industry requires extensive SMS certification driving the need for service providers with safety as a core mission element.

b. *Solar energy farms*—These operations often take place in dry and arid environments, in the middle of fields, on top of large buildings or rooftops, or over large areas with people, infrastructure or vehicles underneath. Systems that have flight termination capability, provide ballistic parachute, or minimize kinetic energy through construction elements or speed/descent reliability may be highly important. Higher population densities require more safety mitigation through operational assessment.

c. *Pipeline and power-line inspection*—All types of regions exist that provide the setting for power-line and pipeline inspection. The areas may be vast and open, enclosed near buildings or infrastructure, or even along cliffs driving the need for UAS inspection in lieu of helicopter or dangerous ground ascent. This may drive fixed-wing or rotor-based design, may require advanced communication shielding, or prevention of R/F interference that only drones developed specifically for the organization's unique needs may contain.

3. Conditions for operations—Wind speed limitations (headwind, crosswind, gust), turbulence restrictions, minimum visibility conditions, outside air temperature limits:

a. *Oil and gas inspections*—Oil and gas installations are found all over the world and in climates from locations in the hottest and coldest regions on the planet. To identify one platform as being able to provide coverage for these locations is impossible. Interfaces that can operate in freezing conditions will not act the same as in bright, sweltering humidity and heat. Air vehicles may require de-icing capabilities, high-wind tolerances, or shielded internal avionics that work in freezing environments. Organizational processes that identify when and how visibility conditions can be accepted for their risk are extremely important and should be made at an organizational level, rather than an operational one. Service providers versus internal organizational operation choices need to be made ahead of time to determine who can take on the appropriate level of risk for weather or environmental happenstance.

b. *Solar inspections and pipeline and power-line inspection*—These elements have similarities when it comes to environment. Whether the conditions are sunny and bright, or cloudy and misting, mission capability may be impacted as the sensor loads (LiDAR, EO, IR) tend to have preferred conditions for efficiency. Understanding when a mission should or should not take place, as well as what sensor load and platform are preferred for condition effectiveness, is vital for creating a meaningful inspection program. Modularity may be a requisite for an organization, or impossible based upon the requirement for training or access to maintainers and integrators on site.

4. Payloads or sensor needs—Configurations, usability, lighting conditions, proximity to scanning environment, clarity and resolution needs, timeline for access to data, data security and management:

    a. *Oil and gas inspections*—Payloads and sensor needs are driven by data requirements and resource investment. ConocoPhillips, Chevron, and Shell seem to have the same needs if you are on the outside looking in, but those who have worked with each of these companies recognize that sub-contractors, manufacturers, and even operational process differ between these companies. Where EO/IR data can be packaged and delivered for one, sensitive data may need to be stored completely differently for another. Set-up of the operations themselves may require different operational approvals, and understanding these dissimilarities is vital to a successful operation.

    b. *Solar energy farms*—While I have not worked directly with solar energy inspections, their sensor needs are clearly evolving. Where once photogrammetry was preferred over LiDAR, 2015 saw the demand for LiDAR increase exponentially. This in turn has driven the development of new LiDAR systems for UAS use such as the Velodyne™ Puck.

    c. *Pipeline and power-line inspection*—Is EO/IR enough? Do analysts at home have the same requirements as those on the ground? Is LiDAR required to make an operation effective or do some inspectors that may require less training simply need visual recognition of deterioration with extensive analytics? Is IR preferred for some infrastructure but necessary for others? As photogrammetry has evolved to nearly 99 per cent effectiveness of sub-liminal LiDAR systems, perhaps developing a photogrammetric system utilizing EO/IR capabilities is more effective in the long term.

5. UAS performance characteristics—Maximum altitude (not regulatory), maximum airspeed, cruise or hover airspeed, maximum endurance, maximum range, maximum rate of climb/descent, maximum bank angle, turn rate limits, payload capacity, battery draw:

    a. *All three types*—In our experience, those tasked with developing programs for UAS inclusion into current operations tend to look at the UAS performance characteristics more so than the rest of the CONOPS. They recognize that the platform is important and believe flight time, distance, speed, battery life, and maximum lift will drive their acquisition decision. While important, we believe it is more important to understand what mission you are trying to accomplish, what data needs exist for that mission, which sensor platform is available that meets those goals, and then decide upon mission length, location, and vehicle.

The energy sector, inclusive of all infrastructure that keeps it running, has the potential to be revolutionized by UAS more so, perhaps, than any other sector. As autonomy grows, regulations become less restrictive or companies begin to understand how to operate within their restrictions, more and more business uses will be discovered and effectively promoted. It will be up to those creating programs now to drive the industry forward as it cannot exceed without corporate entrepreneurs taking risks, betting on progress, and implementing solutions to newly recognized inefficiencies. Later we'll look at the agriculture sector where companies have issues and where they can benefit from better CONOPS development on the front end.

Most importantly, it is in the best interests of all players to go through a methodical and well-understood systems engineering process before taking the irreversible steps of purchase and implementation of UAS.

Some final thoughts on not simply this industry, but all industries:

- Avoid the headaches by remembering integration of back-end software to front-end data acquisition, and how users in your company will effectively use the UAS information.
- Identify your mission needs before you develop the program so you aren't stuck with the wrong platform for the right mission.
- Demand a tailor-made hardware or software solution rather than buy off-the-shelf products with inadequate customer support.
- Use payloads and sensors that make sense for you!

The agricultural buzz—Sensors drive designs

This section of the case analysis looks at the industry that has been the benchmark of unmanned aircraft revolution and one that even consumer-grade manufacturers are beginning to integrate into their portfolio. That industry, of course, is agriculture. If you have been a part of the drone community since 2010 you have heard the promises of AUVSI or industry representatives when it comes to two markets—law enforcement and agriculture. In 2013 AUVSI published an industry-leading analysis on the economic impact of drone integration in an effort to foster investment in the growing drone industry and to provide reasons for lawmakers to minimize regulatory hurdles impeding unmanned innovation. It's no surprise that the stalwart hero of that report was agriculture (Jenkins and Vasigh 2013). Clarion calls for a new agricultural revolution were raised to help feed the people of the world, help the struggling farmer, and accommodate the population booms sure to come in the next decade.

This AUVSI report is one of the most important industry analyses responsible for the rapid adoption by investors and interest by lawmakers. It was coupled with efforts by major manufacturers and industry voices. Expectations were high, and money began pouring in. Unfortunately, the report made the same mistake that many organizations do—they believed one size fits all for farms.

AUVSI got a lot right in that report, but they misunderstood one element that we are still seeing ramifications of to this day in agricultural markets. This report assumed that the adoption rate of UAS technology by farmers in Japan would be the same adoption rate by American farmers, essentially equating the US farmers' needs to Japanese farmers' needs. This reflects the very same assumptions that many manufacturers, consumers, and entrepreneurs take when approaching UAS, and is one of the many pitfalls in business: Needs Must Drive Mission. In fact, the UAS that was so rapidly adopted in Japan and propagated throughout East Asia (Korea, Japan, China) have not found the same use in the United States, mostly because the average farm size in the United States is 444 acres while in Japan the average farm is 4.8 acres and tiered. The terrain and size in Japan are much better suited for UAS and have led to the great success of the Yamaha RMAX™ and other spraying drones.

The Yamaha RMAX™ is a great machine and has delivered much success to Asian farmers due to the size of farms, friendly regulatory environment, and payload capacity of the vehicle. It does not translate well to the American farms, and yet the agricultural revolution promised by drones is not dead in the US. Instead of pesticide and chemical distribution, American farmers have found success using various types of sensor platforms to gather information on their crops and provide a number of targeted, well-defined, environmentally safe solutions. Manufacturers, now seeing their products being utilized by agricultural experts, have begun producing sensors specifically for this market, such as the newly announced Parrot Sequoia with multispectral sensors and luminosity sensor, or the DJI agricultural drone Agras™ focusing on spraying technologies.

There are clear differences in these applications, and knowledge of all elements for new operations including location, environment, training, and mission all play important roles in selecting equipment.

The basic elements of any CONOPS include the following elements, discussed within the context of agriculture:

1. Type of operation—Visual line of sight, extended line of sight, or beyond line of sight:
    a. *Multispectral imaging* and *photogrammetry*—VLOS is where we are, but BLOS and EVLOS operations are where we need to be. Farmers are clamoring to be able to use their SenseFly eBee™ in a BLOS capacity so they don't have to re-deploy or move around from a good take-off and landing site to a potentially risky or sensitive area.
    b. *Spraying*—VLOS is really where spraying operations will remain in the short and medium term. FAA and international guidelines require different standards and operations for volatile or poisonous chemical payloads. This may change, but as it stands, UAS have neither the capacity, battery life, nor support for EVLOS or BVLOS chemical dispersion. Nor is there political support for allowing UAS to deliver anything besides packages.

c. *Herding and livestock monitoring*—BVLOS/EVLOS/VLOS are all in play. This is not just for surveillance, but for surveying, head count, herding, and environmental monitoring. It's clear that this is an in-demand use for UAS and one that will provide lucrative opportunities in the future, once EVLOS and BVLOS are accessible.

2. Definition of flight area and airspace—Population density, expected air traffic, expected surface traffic, types of buildings or vital infrastructure in the area, any confined or obstructed areas, emergency landing areas or terminal flight areas:

a. *All three*—One differentiator for agriculture that has allowed its quick adoption and success is that population density, flight area, traffic in the air and on the ground, and vital infrastructure are minimal and thus considered much lower on the risk spectrum by FAA. Farmers were able to access Section 333 approvals very rapidly and have been able to adopt new technologies at a much more rapid rate than some other industries. Agricultural stakeholders generally have direct control over their environment, can maintain complete control over operations, and provide assurance that they take upon themselves the risk of flight much more so than operations in urban or sub-urban environments.

3. Conditions for operations—Wind speed limitations (headwind, crosswind, gust), turbulence restrictions, minimum visibility conditions, outside air temperature limits:

a. *Multispectral imaging* and *photogrammetry*—Operational considerations always drive mission parameters and understanding how a payload will perform in addition to the air vehicle is very important. Much of the multispectral imaging will not operate effectively or efficiently in cloudy, misty, or otherwise overcast conditions as light diffracts differently and will send different results. This often requires additional calibration. The newest sensors provide calibration in air using luminosity sensors, but understanding when you can operate and the mitigations for success are very important.

b. *Spraying*—Temperature of the soil and the plants themselves, as well as the conditions for payload delivery systems and chemicals, often have certain conditions for optimal results. Wind has a huge impact and it is recommended that a farmer should only spray in winds between 2 and 15kmph and directly into a crosswind. Drift is one of the most important characteristics to understand and a farmer should not believe spraying from a drone is the same as spraying from a manned aircraft.

c. *Herding and livestock monitoring*—Visibility, wind gusts, and temperature all affect herding and monitoring as the animals simply act differently in different conditions. It may not be worth the effort to use UAS in high winds as the sound is the major herding effect and wind tends to deaden any sounds. Icing and other known conditions will also affect flights.

4. Payloads or sensor needs—Configurations, usability, lighting conditions, proximity to scanning environment, clarity and resolution needs, timeline for access to data, data security and management:

   a. *Multispectral imaging* and *photogrammetry*—Payload and sensor needs are the most important elements of agricultural use—the drone is just a flying thing to put a sensor on, after all. The bullet points below should help determine what you need:

      • RGB (red/green/blue): visual inspection, elevation modeling, plant-counting.
      • NIR (near-infrared): soil property and moisture analysis, crop health/stress analysis, water management, erosion analysis, plant-counting.
      • RE (red-edge): crop health analysis, plant-counting, water management.
      • multiSPEC 4C™ (multispectral): both NIR and RE applications, except plant-counting.
      • thermoMAP™ (thermal infrared): plant physiology analysis, irrigation scheduling, maturity evaluation, yield forecasting.[8]

   b. *Spraying*—What types of spraying will you be doing and how does the disbursement mechanism accommodate different varieties of spray? Are you dispersing pesticide or nitrogen? Are you feeding crops or killing pests? Can you go from one to the other? Do you need a new tub completely or can you simply exchange one out? Does the drone allow for easy change? These questions must be answered before you invest in a long-term design.

   c. *Herding and livestock monitoring*—A camera and extra batteries may be the ticket for herding and livestock monitoring. However, you may also want health information from the livestock and therefore EO/IR capabilities may be needed. You may want to create 3D mapping of paths and environment so photogrammetry payloads would be needed.

5. UAS performance characteristics—Maximum altitude (not regulatory), maximum airspeed, cruise or hover airspeed, maximum endurance, maximum range, maximum rate of climb/descent, maximum bank angle, turn rate limits, payload capacity, battery draw:

   a. *Multispectral imaging and photogrammetry*—The trick with imaging is that slow is better than fast so hover time and ease of control are much more important than maximum speeds and altitudes. Imaging and photogrammetry require longer flights from a variety of angles to create the best maps and therefore battery time is king.

   b. *Spraying*—Being so new and really just finding a pathway forward makes determining most important flight characteristics tough. If I were designing the system, I would want to incorporate drift calibration, dispersion automation, and coverage maximization into flight characteristics so that the user must only input directions and locations and the flight computers figure the rest. Likely we're getting close (as this is the main change in imaging control now).

c. *Herding and livestock monitoring*—Flight time, speed, and quick reactions are all important players for the herding and livestock monitoring. As we move into greater levels of automation, systems may be able to intercept wayward flocks without user control. We're not there yet but hey, there is an idea for all you entrepreneurs! It is needed, go do it.

The agricultural industry is leading the way in adoption for much of drone use and will continue to do so as the needs of farmers are met by the capabilities of technology. As my colleague and friend Mitch, whose family have been soy bean farmers for generations, says, "If it doesn't make sense, farmers won't use it." He's exactly right. We must first understand the needs of a system before applying the latest "miracle cure." Drones are a great solution for many problems, but, again, one size does not fit all. Understand your needs or your client's needs and demand a tailored system designed just for you!

6 How to be safe and legal: SMS for remotely piloted aircraft

Safety will be the benchmark that determines how quickly and how successfully unmanned aircraft develop over the next decade. Will close-calls, mishaps, and accidents continue to define the discussion over unmanned aviation, or will UA pilots embrace the lessons learned from both manned and unmanned aviation in a community wide engagement for safety? There are of course some impediments to moving beyond the mere appreciation of safety, or that safety and security are your number one concerns. To fully understand what makes an aviation outfit successful—through safe execution of flights, maintenance, and support operations—we must turn to what has continued to evolve in manned flight.

A wise person once said, "Safety doesn't happen by accident." Safety-focused organizations require commitment from the very top and must permeate through continuing education, daily briefings, and empowered frontline workers to maintain a safety culture that encourages hazard identification and mitigation at all levels of an organization. Not only is this method for ensuring safety the most important, fundamental application of leading safety theory, it is also the basis for international and domestic policy that is required for manned commercial operations, and most likely will extend to unmanned operation in the future. The leading safety organizations in the world, from the most safety conscious industry in the world—manned aviation—are embracing the newest systematic approach to safety promotion and follow-through. This has concurrently pushed the Federal Aviation Administration into willfully adopting SMS as a mandated safety program for Part 91 operators and lately for airport operators. Airport pilot programs for SMS have seen the value through cost reduction, incident and accident rate reductions, and overall system efficiency increases (Ludwig, et al. 2007: 3). This recent adoption brings the FAA in line with what is required by international responsibilities to ICAO as stated earlier in the international regulations section, and reintroduced below.

The International Civil Aviation Organization—the regulatory component of the United Nations overseeing international flight—defines Safety Management Systems (SMS) as a "systematic approach to managing safety, including the necessary organizational structures, accountabilities, policies, and procedures" (International Civil Aviation Organization 2013). Seemingly generic at first, this definition affords companies the opportunity to tailor their SMS program to their own needs. What is required of SMS is that an organization addresses safety concerns in a mathematical way—using collected data to perform meaningful analysis for management policy change. While qualitative analysis can always be used often in unmanned aviation there is such little time in flight, accident or incident report data, or other fleet management information normally involved in analysis for manned aviation, quantitative measures are preferred. Most recent FAA publications, including 14 CFR 107 and other guidance materials for approvals and certification, have demonstrated the willingness for FAA to accept qualitative data and subject matter expertise in lieu of quantitative measures when needed.

Whereas the FAA had generally been seen as the leader in aviation safety throughout aviation history, recently ICAO has taken that mantle for forward-thinking safety vision and progress-based aviation recommended practices. ICAO is now considered to be the highest standard for aviation safety and much of that is because of their current leadership for safety management in the world. Annex 19, the newest annex of the international standards by which international aviation organizations operate, requires a signatory State to establish a State Safety Programme (SSP), "for the management of safety in the State, in order to achieve an acceptable level of safety performance in civil aviation." The requirements included in Annex 19—and paralleled in content and form throughout Annex 6, Annex 8, and Annex 14—outline the main principles that clearly define the Safety Management System:

1. Safety policy and objective.
2. Safety risk management.
3. Safety assurance.
4. Safety promotion.

These four principles are known as the four pillars of SMS and are becoming the most important topics in safety theory and application all over the world. It is important to distinguish between a State Safety Progamme (SSP) and an operator's safety program. The SSP is focused on those entities who are direct signatories to the United Nations and ICAO's civilian aviation administration (for the United States the FAA) to develop and maintain safety policies and objectives, risk management, assurance, and promotion. These entities are called "States," much like our own United States; they reflect government entities which govern individuals (in this case operators) within their jurisdiction. Most often, these "States" manage their aviation industry through a regulatory office known as a civil aviation authority (CAA). Through the CAA, the state must require that operators develop an internal safety program that includes these same four pillars, but also reports and contributes to the State Safety Program as a result. This creates a pyramid of information exchange, and a feedback loop at the State and operator level that ultimately promotes and develops safety all over the world.

If we examine this pyramid of information, we see an important element in the development of aviation safety. First, information is gathered at the individual level—pilots, engineers, other crew members, passengers, etc. Any important information such as incidents or accidents, identified hazards or potential hazards, and basic flight reports are gathered and given to the next level—operator management or executives. Depending on the importance of that information or the organization itself, this reporting mechanism provides the opportunity to sift out unneeded information for reporting. Then, any pertinent information requested by the CAAs, mandatory information such as incident/accident reports, or for unmanned aviation a monthly flight report can be sifted through by the State Safety Program. Any trends analysis across the industry can take place, common hazards or mitigations be recognized, and then information be returned to the public. In essence, safety information is being exchanged first within an organization and then lessons learned passed upwards to the state. The state passes this information on internationally as continuous hazards are identified and the various mitigations which have been used successfully passed on to others. This system of feedback and engagement has helped contribute to a level of safety unparalleled in any other transportation industry, and will be a major support to the unmanned aircraft industry.

The Federal Aviation Administration is only beginning to adopt the tenets of Safety Management Systems in highly specialized areas of the aviation industry. Currently, there is a major push and regulatory effort for the requirement of SMS for airports. The year 2010 saw the beginning of this movement at FAA through the SMS for Certificated Airports Notice of Proposed Rulemaking (NPRM) and the SMS for Part 121 Certificated Holders NPRM (Federal Aviation Administration 2016). The Airports SMS has moved forward while the Part 121 SMS rules have been withdrawn as per docket no FAA-2009-0671. By FAA Order 1110.152, the FAA established the SMS Aviation Rulemaking Committee (ARC) chartered to "provide recommendations to the FAA on the development and implementation of SMS regulations and guidance for aeronautical product/service providers" (U.S. Department of Transportation 2009). In March, 2010, the FAA SMS ARC clearly stated that organizations "certificated pursuant to 14 CFR Parts 21, 119, 121, 125, 135, 141, 142, 145 . . . and 91" should be included in the SMS mandate. The FAA clearly approves of the SMS model for risk management and seeks to maintain or promote safety leadership within the United States. Clearly, the international community and the FAA have seen that SMS is the future of safety development, and will likely be the model for all aviation worldwide.

The question, really, is how long it will take for unmanned aircraft systems to incorporate SMS into their operations. Will there be a mandated application of SMS much like the current regulations airport operators are looking toward and similar to how ICAO has envisioned much of the international standard operation procedures (SOPs), or will the FAA require far less of UAS initially? Does the FAA envision a gradual compliance to ICAO standards moving forward or will the Safety Management Systems be put in place as test sites become operational and data acquisition at a larger level realized? These questions will need to be answered soon. In the meantime, UAS operators should begin to develop SMS for their own programs for two reasons—to continue to promote safety as they operate and to have a system in place which meets the highest legal obligations of a manned commercial aviation operation.

Two problems exist for unmanned aircraft systems integration into the national airspace in the realm of safety. Without question, they are less reliable, do not have the systems testing that manned aviation does, and are known to crash at much higher rates—they incur higher magnitudes of incidents and accidents per flight hour than do manned operations. Without better reliability, and with continued high levels of incident and accident rates, the likelihood of a severe event is high. In this sense, they are by definition a more dangerous, less reliable, form of aviation—encompassing all the same hazardous characteristics of manned flight, with the addition of those added by a lack of co-location of pilots. Vision is limited, conditions in the sky unknown, and you are relegated to flying without tactile, auditory, or olfactory senses in situ. Addressing the inherent flight risks with respect to mechanical, organizational, and social conditions in order to reduce the impact of that inherent risk is the first problem facing UAS operators and one that must be solved through airworthiness certification, business licensing, and private and public scrutiny.

With the understanding that the reliability of such aircraft is much lower than manned aviation, or other systems that humans use for transportation, the other side to the argument is that drones are designed specifically to operate without a human in the vehicle. The aircraft are generally much smaller, much lighter, and composed of very different materials that may not explode or do much damage to something they strike. Their speeds, one could argue, prevent them from doing much damage so that though a crash is more likely, the impact or damage from that crash is expected to be much less severe. This discussion goes directly to the heart of why the unmanned aviation industry will flourish so long as the risk equation discussed ahead is well understood. First, however, we must distinguish between the risk to people and property, and the perceived risk of unmanned aviation in the national airspace.

Perception drives reality in all things, and the unmanned aircraft industry is battling a second main problem of perception by the public. With the understanding that the general public is already weary of privatized "drone" use, the impact of an accident can only be much greater, not less, than that of a similarly sized, similarly damaging accident or incident. Tolerance of accidents or incidents is only made acceptable by verifiable understandings that safety is a large consideration—there must be proof that safety is important, that safety is in the mind of the operator within the entire social framework that allows for operations. To that end, greater compensation and attention to risk mitigation will be necessary for any unmanned operation.

Solving the problem of public perception and adoption is taking a concerted effort by regulatory agencies, government law enforcement, and industry leaders in lieu of clear beneficial recognition of UAS. By adopting advanced, well-documented, data-driven modes of safety promotion, domestic and international organizations can help promote their own safety image while promoting the benefits that unmanned aircraft can bring to society. This fits very well with the SMS framework as it requires the active documentation of hazards by all levels of an organization, the continued and expert analysis of those hazards to assess risk to the system, the documented conclusions of safety investigations, and an expectation of top-down procedural changes to sufficiently eliminate or reduce the hazards to operations that inevitably characterize air operations.

There is precedent as well for the adoption of SMS domestically and internationally through the codifications from FAA and ICAO respectively. The most recent SMS rulemaking activity "would require certain 14 CFR Part 21, 119, 121, 125, 135, 141, 142, and 145 certificate holders, product manufacturers, applicants, and employers to develop and implement SMS" (U.S. Department of Transportation 2009). While these regulations are yet to be published in the Code of Federal Regulations (CFRs), they offer insight into the domestic mentality toward SMS adoption—essentially that SMS is the best way to limit costs while minimizing risks in aviation as well as in other industries such as rail, maritime, and health. Annex 6, Annex 8, Annex 11, and Annex 14 provide that Operations of Aircraft, Airworthiness of Aircraft, Air Traffic Services, and Aerodromes all required incorporating the four pillars of SMS as the core elements of their safety programs—to be used for mitigating risk and evaluating necessary procedural change. The July 2013 edition of Annex 19, a completely new addition to the Annex codifications of ICAO, has the sole purpose of defining precisely what a State Safety Program is, how a SSP will be used, and what components of SMS are to be included in that SSP. Most important is to note that ICAO's inclusion of UAS in Annex 19 signals this new technology as being party to these regulations. By including UAS, for the first time, as regulated by these necessary SMS programs, it follows that ICAO will continue to move toward requiring UAS operators to utilize the same risk mitigation strategies that manned aviators use. Ultimately, ICAO views UAS not as a completely separate type of aviation to be regulated separately, but an extension of current aviation operating procedures and subject to the same safety programs.

ICAO Circular 32-AN/190 lays out, in identical structure to manned aircraft, the future role of SMS for UAS. The circular recognizes that, "Aircraft operating without a pilot on board present a wide array of hazards to the civil aviation system . . . [and] these hazards must be identified and the safety risks mitigated, just as with introduction of an airspace redesign, new equipment or procedure" (International Civil Aviation Organization 2011: 5). It goes on to identify the key concepts of this new safety management as, "a systematic approach to managing safety, including the necessary organizational structures, accountabilities, policies and procedures," and that those concepts are in turn defined by the States Safety Program which must include "safety policies developed based on safety information, including hazard identification and safety risk management." Both manned and unmanned aircraft will require Safety Management Systems and both will be identified in Annex 6, Annex 11, and Annex 14. Circular 32-AN/190 points this out as:

> Assuring the safe introduction of UAS into the aviation system will fall under the responsibility of the State in accordance with Annex 6— Operation of Aircraft, Annex 11—Air Traffic Services, and Annex 14 —Aerodromes, Volume I—Aerodrome Design and Operations.
> (International Civil Aviation Organization 2011: 6)

It is envisaged that Annex 6 will be expanded to include UAS at which point the SMS requirement will become applicable for the UAS operator.

To fully understand why SMS is important, and how it differs from other program management techniques, it is important to address the fundamental theories underlying why SMS is the most successful for transportation industries. SMS addresses important questions relevant to UAS in a uniform way that proactively identifies hazards, looks at the probability of those hazards occurring, and reveals the active risk to the overall systems as a resultant of those hazards. Whether risk is being introduced through newly automated tasks, evolving roles for individuals, or recently designed and attempted missions, human interactions within the system play an important role for the assessment of risk and mitigation of that risk. While a number of models do exist for identifying hazards and mitigating them, it makes sense to adapt the already successful model instituted by aviation leaders and government regulators for use in the UAS industry.

Safety begins from the top. As with any core value defining an organization, the executive leadership must lead the way; it is no different in promoting a safety culture that permeates the whole organization. A safety advisor, responsible for the well-being of pilots, crewman, maintainers, and the public, must have a direct line of communication to upper management. The managers, closer to the frontline operators and engineers, must promote and maintain reporting and data collection through non-punitive reporting procedures that allow everyone from the CEO to the janitors to report hazards they see in their everyday schedules. These managers must encourage individual responsibility as an empowering tool to maintain the highest level of safety assurance, and in turn the frontline operators, understanding that they will not be punished for reporting errors or making honest mistakes, must feel a personal role in creating a safer operating environment. This ideal situation manifests the four pillars of a safety program by developing safety policy and creating a just safety culture, implementing these policies and maintaining open lines of communication, and executing the mitigations through executive support and a dedication to an all-encompassing safety regime. Every person at all levels of the organization is actively engaged and working toward the same goal. Most often, this is defined as maintaining a Just Culture, and is fundamental to a positive, proactive, safety environment.

A culture of safety is vital to diminishing risk, and diminishing risk is mandatory for a UAS company. In order to achieve a meaningful safety culture, the FAA says, you must, "develop [a] process that identifies potential organizational breakdowns and necessary process improvements allowing management to address a safety issue before a noncompliant or unsafe condition results" (Federal Aviation Administration 2010). Traditionally, it has been said that aviation has only learned its lessons when they have been written in blood—meaning that only through a tragic accident, with many fatalities, will risks to the system be taken seriously and prevented from occurring in the future. A proactive approach to risk mitigation has been missing, and the SMS is the highly dynamic and flexible approach to risk mitigation that was needed. The main idea is that SMS improves operations prior to them happening by identifying problem areas through data-driven collection of hazards, close-calls, mishaps, and incidents. When this data is analyzed, problem areas can be identified before they become accidents and cause lives to be lost.

The "old mindset" that is still prevalent in many fields is that "complex systems are inherently safe, we just need to get rid of a few bad apples and everything will be okay" (Dekker 2006: 15). The mindset is that accidents occur because the human element has been introduced to the system, an element that is unreliable, prone to making mistakes and which cannot be satisfactorily mitigated away or reduced satisfactorily. Holders of this mindset believe that there will always be accidents though they should be made to be survivable on an organizational level. This leads to blame and being legal, but not safe. This breeds a focus on compliance to safety guidelines, but not of proactive, systematic hazard identification and mitigation. The underlying assumption is that by complying with laws and regulations and by getting rid of those who commit human errors—"mistakes"—the organization is meeting its legal obligations and thus absolved from further appropriations of resources and time to safety. Unfortunately, this has the effect of ignoring the underlying faults within the system that cause the human to make that mistake. No one comes to work and decides to make an error or cause damage. No one makes a decision in the heat of the moment that they believe is the wrong choice. Therefore, why does it make sense to blame a person, get rid of them, and believe that their choice has now been prevented from happening again? It doesn't. It is likely that the events that created the incident will align again and the same result will occur.

Accidents are not randomly occurring events. Incidents are not the surreptitious whims of fate that have bestowed problems upon your organization. Engineers, operators or managers do not work to create risk or cause damage. The notion, then, that "human error" can be the determinant cause of accident or incidents—and so often is in many investigations—is nonsensical. A person makes a wrong decision for a reason—they were fatigued from flying too many hours or they replaced the wrong part not because they are an idiot but because somehow the system is flawed and in the moment it made sense to replace it as they did. We must determine that underlying problem that appears as human error, before the overall system is safer. As Sydney Dekker puts it, human error ". . . is the effect or symptom, of deeper trouble . . . [It is] not random. It is systematically connected to features of people's tools. Tasks and operating environments . . . [It is] not the conclusion of an investigation. It is the starting point" (Dekker 2006, 18).

No system is completely safe, but UAS are at higher risk for new flaws to arise. UAS have unique characteristics that become prone to "human error." Among these is a third-person approach to flying for those who are used to a first-person approach. Bad information relayed from miscommunications or automation errors is particularly prone to human error issues. Any number of environmental, weather, or crew components lead directly to accidents or incidents that otherwise could be mitigated. It is not, however, the goal to punish or remove flaws. It is the goal of a robust safety program to identify flaws or hazards in the system and ensure they are not repeated. Incidents happen all the time for a variety of reasons—complacency, mechanical failings, maintenance errors, or organizational behavior endemic to all sizes of organizations. By understanding that these will occur, but being prepared to identify them and report them, the system can be flexible and safer. Individuals with proper training can identify problem points before they become incidents or accidents, so long as those individuals are empowered to do so and given the proper understanding of the system overall.

The best way to visualize this, is through James Reason's Swiss Cheese Model. Though there are many layers within the system and each has already identified hazards and mitigated them, new issues arise. Those issues generally

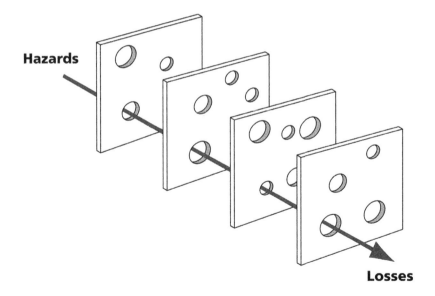

Figure 6.1 James Reason's Swiss Cheese model of aircraft accident causation

do not lead to accidents and rarely do they lead to incidents. However, once in a while—at a ratio generally of 600 incidents to 30 accidents to 10 serious accidents to 1 fatal accident, these hazards align. The goal, then, is not to eliminate all hazards but mitigate those hazards to tolerable levels. You will never be able to eliminate all risk, but you can control that risk and therefore protect your organization and its operations. This book strives to offer the toolset in understanding how that risk can be mitigated through the hazard identification and analysis worksheet and through the FAA's own risk matrix analysis tool. What it all comes down to is simple—severity vs likelihood. The more severe a hazard to the operation and the greater the likelihood, the more important it is to mitigate. Conversely, the less severe a hazard and the less likely it is to occur, the less important it becomes to mitigate. Therefore, the equation used in a SMS Risk Assessment is:

$$\text{Severity} \times \text{Likelihood (probability)} = \text{Risk}$$

Yes, the tool—the equation—seems simple. It seems so simple, in fact, that one wonders why it is necessary at all. It appears as common sense—risk is just the likelihood something happens in conjunction with the severity of that event, and frankly the concept is simple. However, the trick is in understanding the importance of the risk as an output of this function. By acknowledging that the severity of the event and the likelihood of the event occurring are separate characteristics, the risk of the event to the well-being of the overall operation can be deconstructed, better understood and analyzed, and a decision as to mitigation needs and strategies developed. It is this deconstruction and solution strategy that validates and enables the SMS framework.

The hazard identification described earlier acts as a source for probability data as well as severity. As frontline operators—RPA pilots, maintainers, manufacturers, upper management, and safety officers—all report hazards they have encountered patterns and identifiers begin to emerge. If a Phantom 2+ Vision loses GPS signal mid-flight 1 out of every 20 flights that becomes a probability of 5 per cent that a GPS signal loss will occur when flying under trees. If a GPS signal loss mid-flight leads to terminal loss each and every time due to instability and difficult user procedures in taking manual control over the airframe, then the severity of the event is "high." By using the equation above, you would find that 5% of flights conducted below a tree line will have a high risk of failure. The question is how to proceed with that information.

To maximize the use and efficacy of the SMS Risk Assessment model, it is important to understand how determining risk helps an aviation organization. An organization can only survive if it includes risk assessments that are useful for operators to know when to operate, when to check with supervisors as to attaining higher-risk allowances for a mission, or when to scrub the mission entirely and try again another day or use mitigations that will alleviate the high level of risk. Figure 6.2 shows a risk matrix as described by the FAA as to how

Risk Likelihood		Risk Severity				
		Catastrophic A	Hazardous B	Major C	Minor D	Negligible E
Frequent	5	5A	5B	5C	5D	5E
Occasional	4	4A	4B	4C	4D	4E
Remote	3	3A	3B	3C	3D	3E
Improbable	2	2A	2B	2C	2D	2E
Extremely Improbable	1	1A	1B	1C	1D	1E

Figure 6.2 Example risk matrix illustrating the relationship between likelihood and severity

to determine when risk is acceptable or not. Often this matrix brings together both qualitative and quantitative analyses to produce a grid on which events are graphically represented to express quickly and easily where on the spectrum an event may fall. When discussing severity, "worst credible state" in the event of a mishap or accident directly caused by the event is what is being considered. This can be understood to be what is the worst credible outcome for a failure or hazard being considered. A severity score is particularly susceptible to bias or incorrect assumptions, as severity is generally a qualitative analysis of an event and open to interpretation. The FAA requires that all SMS programs include severity as a determinant for event mitigation, but it doesn't specifically define how that severity should be established: the number of lives lost, value of damage lost, etc. It is up to the safety officer or safety program manager to determine these scores, and they are often directly related to cost benefit analysis.

The probability of an event occurring is usually much easier to define as there is significant data available from manufacturers and maintainers as to failure rates and requirements for airworthiness standards. What are less defined are those probabilities of an event driven by human machine interface, communications failures, environmental hazards, organizational flaws, and fatigue. These are just a few of the issues that are uniquely represented with the unmanned systems; making risk assessment even more important using verifiable data acquired through frontline operators (pilots). Probabilities are examined for how often an event occurs based upon acquired data from within an organization via employee debriefings, computer error reporting, accident and incident investigations, security reports, personnel reports, and Transportation System

Wide Reporting sources such as the ASRS (Aviation Safety Reporting System) database run by NASA or ICAO/FAA reports.

As the risk matrix comes together you begin to understand how severity and likelihood work together to determine acceptable or unacceptable risk evaluations. As the likelihood of an event occurring (probability) increases, the threshold for acceptable severity diminishes, while conversely as likelihood decreases severity may increase. In the example risk matrix provided, dark grey is the coded area for acceptable risk—meaning the operation could move forward without mitigation of the event. The white area denotes that mitigation strategies are needed as either the severity or the likelihood of the event make the risk tolerable but in need of mitigation. The light grey means that currently no mitigation can sufficiently diminish the risk to the system and therefore the operation should not move forward until the risk is assessed to be below the "unacceptable" threshold.

AC 107-2 includes a number of parameters that should be assessed prior to operation that directly impact the risk assessment of an operation. An analysis must consist of proper "Aeronautical Decision-Making (ADM);" a process that addresses all aspects of decision-making in a solo or crew environment. ADM also includes methods for making good decisions and communicating those decisions throughout all active parties. While assessing risk, individual behaviors of PICs, VOs, and any other crew member must be examined ahead of time to include personal attitudes that may be hazardous to safe flight, behavior modification techniques, and recognition and methods to cope with stress (Federal Aviation Administration; AFS-800 2016). Individuality matters and to a great degree the idiosyncrasies of pilots and VOs are tolerable. It is when these individual behaviors trend toward negatively impacting an operation that they must be addressed. Hazardous behaviors can develop in any operation.

Risk mitigation strategies and safety assurance for sUAS

Identifying hazards and evaluating them for their risk characteristics is a huge step forward in providing your operation with the knowledge needed to prevent incidents and accidents, and to cultivate an organizational appreciation for safety. However, simply identifying and understanding that the risks exist does not directly mitigate those risks to a tolerable level. Identification is simply the first step in providing your organization with increasing safety, and enabling you to cultivate a greater appreciation for the limitations in your operation.

Risk management can be called a number of different things. Your organization may reference mitigation techniques or strategies, safety control methods, or incorporate more advanced techniques that follow a system engineering approach, such as Boolean logic gates or fishbone analysis to identify weak points in risk strategies and to provide increasingly appropriate protections. At its core, risk mitigation is intended to do two things directly related to the risk characteristics identified in the risk analysis phase of Safety Management Systems:

- Reduce and/or eliminate the likelihood of a hazardous event occurring.
- Reduce and/or eliminate the severity of a hazardous event if it were to occur.

Clearly these two purposes are intimately linked with the risk matrix and scoring in the risk analysis phase of the UAS flight safety process. By eliminating the likelihood of the event occurring, the approach to safety promotes an overall greater safety condition by strategizing to eliminate risk to an operation associated with the event ever occurring. If the event were to occur, however, the effect on the overall system would be the same, or possibly greater, as complacency or belief that the event can never occur may lessen or negate reactions to the event. Examples of strategies that may address the likelihood (or probability) of the event occurring would be:

- Installing more powerful communication technologies or redundant systems that will reduce the likelihood that lost-link occurs leading to a catastrophic incident.
- Enforcing a policy or procedure that limits the overall flight time of a pilot to less than 5 flights per day for no greater than 30 minutes per flight in order to reduce or eliminate flight fatigue as a root cause for incidents.
- Enforcing a policy or procedure that requires a full battery be installed prior to every flight in order to reduce the likelihood that the flight will be impacted by low battery.
- Enforcing a procedure requiring VOs to visually check the airframe after the PIC does in order to reduce the likelihood that a structural flaw exists prior to flight.
- Enforcing a policy or procedure that allows for randomized drug testing (if allowed by your company) to reduce the likelihood that PICs or VOs fly under the influence of alcohol or narcotics.
- Enforcing a policy or procedure that enables any employee to report an incident anonymously without fear of retribution from management in an effort to identify hazards before they become accidents.

Examples of strategies that may address the severity of an event occurring could be:

- Installing a ballistic parachute that, if an emergency situation were to occur, would limit the terminal velocity of the airframe in order to minimize the kinetic energy in an accident.
- Requiring PICs to designate an emergency landing position far away from people or property on the ground in order to reduce the severity of a crash.
- Limiting the weight characteristics of the airframe to only what is needed through purchasing decisions and mission tasking in order to reduce the kinetic energy at impact on the ground.

- Enforcing a policy or procedure that promotes proper battery maintenance and handling in order to promote fuel cells' health onboard any sUAS flight.
- Enforcing a policy or procedure that limits the maximum speed, altitude, or range to only what is needed for the operation will also limit the kinetic energy profile associated with an incident or accident caused during flight, and therefore any flight should take into consideration this easy and quick severity-limiting approach.

Safety risk management has been studied for decades and has directly impacted the safety of aviation throughout the world. As it applies to sUAS, there are common developing techniques that enable safer flight in and around a capacity of operations and environments. Personal experience has shown that each industry has unique hazards inherent to its operations that require increasingly complex knowledge. The energy sector, ripe for innovative approaches to solving inspection problems, has also illustrated unique challenges. Power-line inspections come with unique conditions that must be considered by operators prior to flights. Electro-magnetic interference that can cause lost-link procedures when coming close to transformers or towers of different sizes provide a need for policies, procedures, and training that consider such environmental issues. These challenges increase the likelihood of an incident occurring, and the proximity to vital assets and sensitive areas increases the severity associated with a crash. In response, a UAS safety advisor or PIC in the field would need to identify a buffer for proximity to the power-line, provide warning signals that may require the operation to "move-back," or denote instances where or when the operation could move forward.

Mitigation strategies must also be appropriate to the operation taking place and not create any risks that were otherwise non-existent prior to the mitigation. A mitigation strategy that creates further risks is not a valid strategy, and therefore risk mitigation strategies must always be analyzed in accordance with the original hazard identification process. It should be remembered that change is a hazard as it usually requires training, policy adaption, manualization and documentation, and approvals and therefore before any change is finalized, it must be assessed for likelihood and severity as any other hazard would be in aviation. Residual risk can be just as dangerous for an operation as initial risk associated with hazards. By changing an operation to minimize one risk, you can create higher risks. An example of this can be changing the flight environment from directly over houses (not allowed in many operational approvals) to flying directly over a power-line. Ultimately crashing into a roof would not be positive and may require a report to the FAA based on the outcome, but flying into a power-line and knocking out power to tens of thousands of people would be far worse. This residual risk would not be tolerated even if the operational approval is permitted by regulations. In this instance, the risk analysis would illustrate that the resulting risk score would not be less than the initial hazard, and a new mitigation would be required prior to flight.

Safety assurance, the pillar of SMS that the FAA recognizes as encompassing evaluation of the overall system, provides "insight and analysis regarding methods/opportunities for improving safety and minimizing risk." Coupled with the risk mitigation component, an organization is able to use data and reporting methodologies to factually track and assess the operational provisions and limitations they impart through policies, procedures, training, and documentation. What is missing, however, is still a good methodology for ensuring the organization maintains a positive safety culture and appreciation for risk assessment, mitigation, and continuous proactive self-evaluation. This aspect can be found through safety promotion.

In the interest of assuring safe practices, the following methodologies are industry standards and should be included in any safety program:

Inspections—The organization will conduct internal evaluations of the operational processes and systems at planned intervals to determine if the safety program is continuing to meet the needs of the organization and overall safety goals. Maintenance and inspections processes, checklists for quality control, airframe and component lists, ground control condition, parts and material control, documentation and technical data management should all be inspected for continuity and appropriateness. Inspections should also include:

- Certification and qualification systems.
- Training requirements and performance records.
- Flight operations data and documentation.

Audits—Verifying compliance with the operations manual, standard operating procedures, and the expectations of the organization is vital to ensuring that the safety program is functioning effectively. Audits are an integral component to any safety program and must cover all aspects of operations, support, and infrastructure to ensure completeness.

An accountable executive or manager involved intimately with the operation and overseeing safety will ensure regularly scheduled internal audits. The CSO may delegate evaluation to inspectors for the auditing process, though the CSO is responsible for the following:

- Scheduling and communicating audit evaluations.
- Recording and reporting results to personnel.
- Maintaining documentation relevant to the audit.

Safety audits will cover the following areas and evaluate them for relevance, effectiveness, organizational structure, and impact:

- Safety policy and safety culture.
- Key personnel and their functions responsible for safety.

- Effectiveness of hazard identification.
- Risk management process success.
- Safety assessment procedures and documentation.

Investigations—Mishaps, incidents, accidents, and other events must be investigated as required in all certification documentation and reports developed as needed and in cooperation with authorities. Information gathered in the course of these investigations is a vital source for accident prevention and is the true goal. Each safety investigation should be led by a representative manager for the safety program and include the following elements:

- Analysis focused on determining the "root cause" of the event, under-standing that "human error" is not usually a root cause, but reminiscent of systematic flaws that lead to an active error.
- An analytical and systematic approach to accident causation that should determine causal, contributing, and latent factors/hazards that contributed to the event.
- A detailed report of all findings that includes specific recommendations for reducing either the likelihood or the severity, or both, of the event, in the future.

Performance monitoring, data analysis, change management—Understanding safety impacts through monitored change, and data that reflects a need for change, is only helpful in an environment in which change can be managed and new hazards that may arise identified as before. With any organizational, operational or procedural change, new hazards may arise and therefore a process for addressing those is extremely important.

The following requirements should define the change management and performance monitoring platform within the safety program:

- Identify any new hazards that may arise from any change, and assess that hazard for new risk to the operation.
- Identify any need for new procedure, process, or checklist item that may mitigate that risk if the risk is deemed unacceptable.
- Follow a documented management process in order to update the policies or procedures with changes as needed.
- Follow a training manual change management process in order to update that document with changes as needed.

Safety promotion for sUAS operations

Safety promotion is one of the most difficult components of SMS and is where training and leadership drive change directly. Through constant self-evaluation, proactive hazard identification and risk mitigation the organization is continu-ously made safer. However, this system can only achieve greater results through the constant appreciation for safety. If an operator begins to feel pressured to perform at the cost of safety or less reporting, the entire system is made less safe. One incident or accident can lead to another, and the reputation of a company is imperiled. Safety promotion helps to solve this problem in a number of ways, but new methods are developed by each and every organization. Likewise, some methods for promoting safety within one company may not apply or be too resource-focused to be applicable to another.

Safety promotion requires the combination of training and communication specifically geared toward safety information between employees, management, and contractors. Your goal in safety promotion is to enhance your company's safety performance. You are not trying to limit liability or promote economic performance. Your only goal in safety promotion is safety. How you determine that your company can exceed expectations and grow your safety bottom line is up to you; however, there are a number of foundational thoughts that should ground any and all safety promotion efforts. These efforts, according to the FAA, include promoting a positive safety culture, involving management, competency and training, and communication.

- *Positive safety culture*—Much has been said about positive safety culture. An organization that defines its success through the lens of safety performance promotes voluntary reporting of incidents and accidents, and encourages its employees to truly embrace safety as a core function of their roles to create better communication and empower their entire organization. Positive safety culture must start at the top, and therefore having an accountable executive who understands the importance of each individual working together is vital.
- *Involving management*—By ensuring that all levels of management embrace safety as the single most important element of the operation and that operators, VOs, maintainers, and purchasers also embrace that role. Creating weekly or monthly meetings in which management and operators interface, with a complete focus on safety performance and other operational items promotes that open communication necessary to positive safety culture and promoting safety.
- *Competence and training*—Recurrent training, safety stand-down days, annual review of performance statistics and flight hours, and a review of reported hazards are all good elements of a robust safety promotion regime. There is more, however, that can be done in the interest of safety promotion, including tasking operators and VOs with external reviews of systems, embracing conference attendance where operators can interface with one another to learn industry best practices, and the adoption of training time beyond operational environments.
- *Communication*—Ensuring that all employees feel comfortable reporting hazards, incidents, or accidents is not easy, and safety promotion is intended to facilitate those discussions by breaking down the silos and walls that can grow in any organization. It does not help an organization to identify

hazards, assess their risk, and mitigate them if those strategies are not disseminated to the entire crew. If an endangered hawk species is seen in an operational area one day, it should be vocalized throughout the organization to help others plan ahead for future operations and to allow management to make informed decisions along the way.

In personal consultation with companies, the following methods for safety promotion are often highly effective and encouraged due to low cost, less intuitional approval requirements, and minimal resources. In other words, these techniques do not expose your company to more risk, but do promote organizational quality, and encourage information exchange with minimal cost:

- *Safety priority top 5*—High priority factors that have been identified to contribute to risk in the operational environment should be identified based on data obtained through the risk assessment process as described. The Top 5 should be communicated to all involved in flight operations including PICs, VOs, schedulers, and program managers. The Top 5 may alternatively be discussed monthly or as needed.
- *Industry lessons learned*—Through research, partnerships, and other industry involvement, leadership should actively describe deficiencies that have been identified by other organizations (including utility companies, manufacturer's regulators, academia, etc.) as having a negative safety effect on UAS operations. These deficiencies should be addressed and potential strategies identified through monthly safety meetings with all SDG&E personnel. Standard operating procedures will be adjusted accordingly and communicated.
- *Are you fit to fly?*—The question "Are You Fit to Fly?" should be asked of every pilot, before every mission in an effort to mitigate the effect of fatigue risk. If the true and honest answer is "No," a new pilot will be found and assigned or the hazard present by fatigue risk will be mitigated to an acceptable level.
- *Training*—Ongoing training designed and reviewed by the Chief Safety Officer should focus on UAS PIC, VO, support staff, and any and all personnel directly related to operations. This may also include personnel directly responsible for maintenance, software update, purchasing, and security. Training is the most recognized and accepted form of safety promotion.

Case study: Risk assessment checklist for sUAS operations

Implementing a risk assessment checklist is one of the most important, easiest, and long-lasting procedures that any company can do to help produce increased safety for the UAS flight team. By including those elements that are identified by the FAA, ICAO, and other safety partners as vital to an operation's long-term safety, individuals can perform better within a context of safety compliance and in respect and appreciation for regulatory requirements.

Luckily, the FAA recently published AC 107-2 which outlines the very basics for a sUAS operation. Building off this framework, an inspection and risk assessment pre-flight checklist can be created that not only goes above and beyond the basic requirements, but also creates a document that is useful, easy to apply in the field, and develops a pathway forward for operational approvals beyond. Internationally these same steps can be included to meet the standards throughout EASA, CASA, and other organizations.

For the purpose of ease of use and applicability across industries, the latest checklist examples and baseline for the industry as of January 2017 are included here. These, of course, derive from those included in the FAA Advisory Circular 107-2. While not intended to be considered comprehensive enough to allay any development, analysis, or creation on the part of the reader's organization, it is a great start to meet compliance with FAA activities through 107 and begin the process-oriented approach toward institutional checklist development.

Table 6.1 sUAS Operations Checklist

Phase of flight and notes	Item	Status
Flight assignment	NOTAM Filed Identified safety items briefed to designated PiC	
Prior to departure to operation site	Aircraft (AC) and Remote Control (RC) Battery % Checked Tablet Charged to Appropriate % Portable Radio Charged to Appropriate % Frequency (FX) for Operational Area Programmed to Portable Radio Firmware Updated on AC and RC SD Card contains Appropriate Free Space (Blank) Weather Conditions Allow for Operations (<22 MPH Winds, >500' Cloud Layer, 1 mile Visibility, Sunrise/Sunset Times)	
On-site check	Area Free of Overhead Obstructions Wireless Interference appears minimal Weather Conditions Confirmed On-Site On-Site Safety Briefing Conducted	
Physical aircraft check	Positioning Camera is Free of Dirt or Debris Black cable, Red/Black Cable Connected Motors Clear of Foreign Object Debris (FOD) SD Card is in Camera Camera is Mounted According to Manufacturer Guide UAS Tracker Turned On Propellers free from Metling or Cracks and Spin Easily Propellers are Hand Tight Prop Locks Firmly Attached	
Remote controller check	Antennas Oriented Properly Appropriate Flight Mode Landing Gear Switch Oriented Down RC Battery Level at a Minimum of 75%	

Table 6.1 continued

Phase of flight and notes	Item	Status
DJI GO APP *interface* *for PiC*	Maximum flight altitude Set to 500'	
	Fail safe mode set for 3.3' Clearance above Highest Obstacle	
	RC Signal Lost set to Return-to-Home According to Pre-Flight Briefing Location	
	Ensure Batteries are at 90% or Higher	
	Place Camera in FPV position	
	Ensure Satellites are Locked According to Risk matrix (Recommended 12)	
	Face AC into the Wind	
	Check Heading of AC is true to Physical Positioning	
	Start Propellers using a Combined Stick Command (CSC)	
	Callibrate Aircraft According to manufacture Specifications	
	Ensure Blue Dot Representing RC is Accurately Located on Map	
	Ensure Home Point is Accurately Set on Map	
	Ensure Elevation Reads Zero (0)	
In-Flight *Operations*	Follow Operations in Accordance with AOM	
Post-Flight	Ensure Video has Stopped Recording	
	Note Battery Life for both AC and RC	
	Power Off Aircraft	
	Detach Camera and Gimbal, then Store	
	Detach Propellers and Store	
	Power On Aircraft	
	Transition Airframe to Travel Mode	
	Power Off Aircraft	
	Power off Remote Control and Interface	
	Fillout Incident/Accident Report as Needed	
	Debrief	

Lessons learned in blood must not be forgotten: An interview with Thomas Anthony

Academics, government officials, consumers, end-users, and hobbyists all share a passion for the evolving world of unmanned systems. They also all bring varying viewpoints and backgrounds to this divergent industry seeking to become profitable, apply knowledge and understanding to technology that rapidly iterates. All participants in this industry have something to offer, but none more so than those individuals who can understand, appreciate, and synergize viewpoints into meaningful policy and insight. Thomas Anthony is one of those stalwart innovators in the field of unmanned systems with a background and understanding focused in safety and security in manned aviation, founded in his background as an Air Traffic Controller, a FAA Security Regional Manager, a security inspector who worked to help crack terrorist threats in the Pacific Region, and the Director of the University of Southern California, Viterbi

School of Engineering, Aviation Safety & Security Program. It is his insight and visionary approach to aviation education that enabled the creation of the world-leading Safety Management Systems for Remotely Piloted Aircraft course, and his ongoing pursuit to drive forward human factors and crew resource management training for both manned and unmanned aviation.

Director Thomas Anthony helps his students, media representatives, and operators understand the role, impact, and approaches of international organizations, domestic regulators, and academics. His approach is one that so many unmanned systems professionals seem to forsake, approaching this new industry with the lessons learned from aviation and applying them in a commonsense approach or change those that don't seem to fit. In the context of manned aviation, Director Anthony acknowledges, ". . . we have had about 100 years to discover the hazards by means of crashes and near misses. We must use those lessons learned and apply them where we can to avoid them in manned and unmanned aviation moving forward." While certainly there are differences between manned and unmanned aviation, the most important thing to remember, he says, is to recognize that these new aviators are not entering a new world, just using a new tool. "Unmanned aircraft," he says,

> are the evolution of the microcircuit, electronics, and lithium ion batteries all coming together, allowing RPAs and small drones to evolve. Aviation has always been something new. It hasn't ever been something average and it has always captured the inspirational spirit. It's a very fruitful environment for individuals to do the right thing. You can look back and see the Wright Brothers. They weren't just doing something average. They were bicycle builders with an idea. If you look at Charles Lindbergh, he had a vision and did it down in San Diego. To Billy Mitchel, the entrenched military establishment said, "you can never sink a battleship with an airplane," but he proved you could do it. This has always been an area where leadership can make a huge difference, and those of us are doing that now by applying safety to UAVs.

For Director Anthony, safety and security trumps all else in keeping this new industry successful. Without a safe or secure foundation, the industry won't be sustainable. "The idea," he asserts:

> is that instead of following with an evolution cycle of crash fix, crash fix, crash fix, we want to act proactively. We are in an optimum circumstance to implement safety management systems, whereby we can identify hazards through hazard reports and incidents, and through digital data. We can evolve a faster and much higher level of safety for the UAV community, instead of a "crash to fix" mentality that we see in manned aviation.

This "crash to fix" mentality is precisely the problem, and is the focus of proactive safety approaches included throughout this book. It is the culmination of safety theory and leadership over the last few decades, but it is not easy.

This application and implementation of SMS, the proactive safety approach now in favor by ICAO and the FAA, still will require immense buy-in from industry and regulatory leadership. "Ideally," Director Anthony agrees,

> ICAO would serve as the leaders as they so often have in manned aviation for SMS, though ICAO seems to be taking a back seat for SMS for small UAVs and it is really relying upon those contracting states to see the applicability of SMS to small UAVs. It is the small states that are taking the lead and operators who are pushing the state safety programs.

Recently, Randy Willis, the FAA representative to ICAO outlined a roadmap for an SMS recommended practice for UAS operators at the ICAO level by 2017, but would likely only be for the higher categories of UAS. "ICAO," he acknowledges:

> is rightfully much more concerned with the large air carriers, and in a way it is much less natural for them to take a lead for aviation that will generally not be flown internationally; small UAS are least likely to fly across borders and are therefore not the main concern for ICAO.

Ultimately, it will come down to leadership from signatory states to ICAO, national regulators, and commercial entities all working together with industry standards groups that will move us closer to the safety needs.

Meanwhile, Director Anthony appreciates the direction that much of the law enforcement and oil and gas UAS operators are taking as it comes to SMS implementation. "Where we're seeing the most SMS incorporation," Mr. Anthony begins,

> is in the dull, dirty, dangerous, missions. It is these practitioners who have embraced SMS that are leading the way for the industry and where we will see success and failure, and it will be those that adopt SMS early that will lead the safety world.

These operators, especially those operating in high-risk environments or with organizations that have had to place safety as the number one priority already, will have the best safety records, the easiest time access certifications and approvals for operations, and eventually will be the most sought out.

Speaking about the role of stakeholders in the UAS industry, Director Anthony asserts that, "Academia has a unique responsibility to develop new ideas, presenting them and getting them out there, and supporting and promoting them to the regulators and private companies." He believes that often, "regulators exist within the context of large bureaucratic organizations that are influenced heavily by the industry themselves. Academia by its very nature is less beholden to these financial interests and therefore has the ability to speak freely and objectively," to bring real positive change with the latest information and research. Mr. Anthony sees the problems facing the drone community and industry as one that real education and leadership can solve. "The average drone user can realize that there is a national airspace system. A little learning goes a long way. It's all about preparation, preparation, preparation." He believes that ultimately unmanned systems will flourish when those operating them have an understanding of their flight environment. He believes:

> Preparation is what makes a general aviation flight and commercial flight safe. The more you read and the more you prepare; understand the flight rules; the battery state of your aircraft; the more you expand your knowledge and the safer you are. Developing checklists, understanding your environment, is the real key to safety and success in all aviation.

Director Anthony is probably best known for his leadership in applying subconscious or peripheral recognition of hazardous events to interpretation in manned aviation, but he believes that these same lessons can be applied to unmanned aircraft flight. He teaches that certain sensations, though vocalized or felt subconsciously, can be recognized as indicators of negative sensations and those can be used to avoid incidents or accidents.

> Sensations of "huh" often are the recognition of a relationship basically at the subconscious level. The "AHAH" is a large epiphany and "huh" is a small one. It is involuntary, you don't think it through. It comes to you and makes an emotional impact. In a new environment, in a new situation, like working with UAVs, this is a world or community that is full of opportunities for discoveries. It is so new where these "ahah" moments or "huh" sensations come as a result of a realization. That realization can be used to avoid accidents.

This new approach and understanding of threats and errors in flight is perhaps the next evolution of what today is required curriculum in the Human Factors in Aviation (HFH) or Threats and Error Management (TEM) courses often taught at aviation safety schools. Director Anthony is the first to apply that same knowledge to unmanned aviation.

What we can learn from Director Anthony's approach to UAS is that learning lessons from manned aviation is essential as integration moves forward internationally. If we ignore the lessons learned in blood, from vulnerabilities in the past, we will be doomed to repeat them. The industry may not be able to suffer a setback of multiple casualties in its nascent stage, and therefore applying knowledge from any source is vital. SMS, CRM, TEM lessons may hold the key to providing the situational awareness education requisite to flying safely, but it is certainly not enough. Regulators, academics, legislators, and commercial operators will have to collaborate to foster the knowledge needed for the future of UAS, and the full integration of aviation.

7 The States Act and privacy implications for drones

The Federal Aviation Administration was granted sole responsibility to oversee and regulate the airline industry and the national airspace for both military and commercial aircraft in the Federal Aviation Act of 1958 (United States Congress 1958). Since then, it has become the world leader in safety promotion and regulation of airspace and has helped drive similar levels of success throughout Europe. Civil aviation throughout the world has modeled operations, standards, regulations, and structure after the FAA. The International Civil Aviation, in their 2012 ICAO Safety Audit recognized that North America—largely run by the Federal Aviation Administration—was the only UN region to have zero fatal crashes and was the second lowest in accident rates for the year (International Civil Aviation Organization 2012). The FAA has been solely responsible for managing airspace access for over 50 years, and yes it has been tasked by Congress, yet again, to integrate new technology, unmanned aircraft, safely.

The Federal Aviation Administration Modernization and Reform Act of 2012—H.R. 658—empowered Congress to "develop a comprehensive plan to safely accelerate the integration of civil unmanned aircraft systems into the national airspace system," not later than "270 days after the date of enactment [February 14, 2012]" (U.S. Congress, House of Representatives 2012). To accomplish this goal, the FAA was tasked with defining "acceptable standards for operation and certification of civil unmanned aircraft systems . . ." and to establish "standards and requirements for the operator and pilot of civil unmanned aircraft systems, including standards and requirements for registration and licensing" (U.S. Congress, House of Representatives 2012). It is quite clear that Congress, seeing the FAA as the preeminent agency in aviation, granted responsibility to them to lead integration within the United States. Many deadlines and recommendations were outlined in the FAA Modernization and Reform Act of 2012, but none is more important than that which necessitates the provision "for the safe integration of civil unmanned aircraft systems into the national airspace system as soon as practicable, but not later than September, 30, 2015." These mandates have been updated in recent congressional reauthorizations, signed into law in 2016; however, the FMRA of 2012 is clearly the empowering legislation most relevant to the story of UAS development and integration in the United States.

Recognizing that in the case of national airspace regulation, federal law pre-empts state law, many states decided to act prior to the September 30, 2015 deadline. These groups believed that by acting before the FAA acted, they could make an argument establishing the tenth amendment as giving them the power to regulate in lieu of deference from the FAA to act—essentially the argument goes, because the FAA has not acted, the states are left to act. This argument holds little substance as Congress and the FAA are moving forward with the belief that this new technology must be integrated safely, securely, and with great respect to the current national airspace system. Acting prematurely would be much worse to all parties than acting out of fear or ignorance, and in order to create reasonable regulatory framework, time, stakeholders, and technology need to develop.

Meanwhile, the Certification of Authorization system (COA) was being used for all parties interested in flying UAS in the NAS. These COAs allowed the FAA to closely monitor and understand all UAS activity in pre-designated airspace—other than that of the hobbyist and non-compliant commercial community who flourished over the last five years. This process for flight planning and approval grew steadily over the past 4 years culminating in 5,551 Section 333 petitions granted as of September 2016. The advent of the Section 333 system (which includes COA approvals), and the production of the test site approvals convoluted the precise number of authorized and actively operating UAS for commercial purposes in the United States. The system for attaining these COAs may still be online, open to both the public and law enforcement agencies, but not truly open to commercial operations other than two operations granted to Insitu and Aerovironment, both taking place in Alaska and both utilizing a special airworthiness certification before any other commercial operations (Hsu 2013).

The 2012 Reauthorization Bill also directed the FAA to "allow a government public safety agency to operate unmanned aircraft weighing 4.4 pounds or less" under very specific conditions—under 400ft above ground, more than 5 miles from any airport, only during daylight, and inside class G airspace (U.S. Congress 2012). It was the intention of Congress, the FAA, the Justice Department, and all other federal entities that operations move forward using small UAS and large UAS in the national airspace. With this in mind, it was disingenuous to develop regulations in an attempt to usurp or circumvent the federal government's responsibilities. That is exactly what the state governments did, and are doing, in lieu of final regulation by the federal government for all UAS and all UAS operations. It would also appear that though the FAA has published a final rule set, 14 CFR 107 and hope to continue to provide guidance for airspace, states continue to attempt legislation which will limit operations. This continuation changes rapidly and it is likely that even with rapid updates to this book, out of date material will be included. It is up to the reader to see what state legislation is pending.

A great source to maintain up-to-date information with regard to state legislation can be found updated by AUVSI (http://2016-state-uas-legislation.

silk.co/). The state legislative information to follow illustrates the initial round of state measures that often attempted to limit, but in some cases support, UAS programs and operations by the public, law enforcement, or any number of institutional organizations. Some have been overturned, many more have been proposed, but these initial legislative initiatives illustrate the mistrust and misguided approaches legislatures shared throughout the United States toward automated systems.

It is very clear that the states do not have the regulatory power to limit access to unmanned aircraft operating in the national airspace any more than manned aircraft operating in the national airspace. However, there may be room for states to restrict certain types of activities or uses of these aircraft in the national airspace for privacy concerns or within the context of landing and taking off. Except for Virginia's state legislature which opted to limit law enforcement access to airspace, all other states have initially taken an approach limiting the use of information gathered during aerial operations.

As "drones" have emerged as a highly productive technology platform for a variety of industries, many interested parties operate within a vacuum of regulations. While many believe that law enforcement is the main focus and requires the most attention for privacy concerns, in fact many commercial interests exist that deserve attention. Early on, state legislatures have addressed two main concerns defining the debate—safety and privacy. Beginning with Virginia's HB 2012 and SB 1331, states have begun to codify legislation relating to UAS, generally falling into three separate categories:

1. Limiting the use of drones.
2. Defining, expanding, and limiting the role (but not access) of drones.
3. Supporting the expansion of drone research and support in the state.

Virginia's HB 2012 approved April 3, 2013, was the first state legislation in the nation to address unmanned aircraft systems and to define when, where, or why they could operate. The General Assembly of Virginia enacted a moratorium in which "No state or local government department, agency, or instrumentality having jurisdiction over criminal law enforcement regulatory violations . . . shall utilize an unmanned aircraft before July 1, 2015" (Virginia Commonwealth House of Delegates 2013). Still pertaining to law enforcement, the code goes on to identify when restrictions against UAS do not apply such as "Amber Alerts," "Blue Alerts," "for the purpose of a search or rescue operation where use of an unmanned aircraft system is determined to be necessary," or for "training exercises related to such uses." This section, however, does not limit drone usage to search warrants. Further, this legislation directly applies to any access to the national airspace rather than the outcomes of those operations. This conflicts with all other passed legislation in the nation. The "characteristics" of the operations are often identified as the main issue with UAS—privacy concerns stemming from inappropriate or illegal usage of pictures, videos, sound recordings, or other forms of surveillance.

This legislation quite clearly prevents any access to the national airspace by only law enforcement users without acknowledging why they are being banned, or addressing the public use of unmanned aircraft.

This is a relatively common occurrence with state legislation. Often, law enforcement is the direct subject of the legislation being passed in order to allay the fears of citizens over privacy invasion and surveillance.

HB 2012 also makes exceptions for the Virginia National Guard, enabling unmanned aircraft systems during training for, "Federal missions . . . to include damage assessment, traffic assessment, flood stages, and wildfire assessment . . . [and that] nothing herein shall prohibit use of unmanned aircraft systems solely for research and development purposes by institutions of higher education and other research organizations or institutions." Any academic research or federal mission is not forbidden through July 1, 2013 when incorporating UAS. It is out of fear of an invasion of privacy that these regulations were created though there is very little difference between manned and unmanned aviation that may impact the privacy of individuals from law enforcement. The difference between manned and unmanned aviation platforms is mainly the ease of use and the cost of use. Does this satisfy a higher level of scrutiny from manned aviation?

Being the first state to act in limiting the access and use of unmanned aircraft systems has hurt the effectiveness of Virginia's HB 2012 and SB1331. The scope of the legislation went beyond anything other states have attempted to do in limiting airspace access and may be unconstitutional as it limits access of public use entities (state and federal law enforcement) rather than activity. A different approach, embraced by state legislatures throughout the nation, is limited to the types of activities and recordings the UAS are allowed to participate in. This represents less concern constitutionally for the state as it is not limiting access to airspace; the role apportioned solely to the FAA. This approach reduces privacy concerns for its citizens—a role which has not been apportioned to any regulatory body, while still supporting industry development and law enforcement functions.

Idaho, Florida, and Montana offer the greatest insight to the states that have acted similarly to limit the fears of privacy invasion that UAS may represent. While at the time of this writing there have been 9 states that have passed "anti-UAS legislation" and 19 more that have been defeated, these three act as the templates for the "anti-UAS" states (Mairena and Davis 2013). These states have acted in a more uniform effort to prevent the use of images, sounds, video recordings, or other UAS mounted technologies such as infrared or hyper-spectral analysis. Unique in these approaches is that they clearly identified the product of the flight (the pictures, videos, etc.) as being unlawful as evidence unless attained through the execution of a search warrant, when in the protection of society from a terrorist event, and other very specific situations. They are targeting, therefore, the use of data, rather than the manner by which the data is acquired. This is an important distinction.

Idaho limited UAS activities by first splitting the definition of what defines unmanned aircraft. Idaho excluded "model flying airplanes or rockets . . . that are radio controlled or otherwise remotely controlled and that are used purely for sport or recreation . . ." as well as "unmanned system(s) used in mapping or resource management" (Idaho State Senate 2013). By this definition, Idaho, excludes two of three of the main users of drones from their legislation—hobbyists and agriculture/urban planning—opening the skies to all but law enforcement. The law does allow law enforcement the use of drones, "absent a warrant" or in "emergency response for safety, search and rescue, or controlled substance investigations" (Idaho State Senate 2013). These are core functions of law enforcement that are all excluded from legislation. Only the use of "unmanned aircraft system(s) to intentionally conduct surveillance of, gather evidence or collect information about, or photographically or electronically record specifically targeted persons or specifically targeted private property" by law enforcement is disallowed—without a warrant. With a warrant, these activities are allowed. Finally, non-law enforcement photography is limited to prior consent for the purpose of publishing specifically. It is clear that Idaho—recognized as the second most limiting state for UAS activities behind Virginia—is acting to limit the use of UAS photographic and sound recording, but not limit the activity of flight.

Florida's SB 92 was enacted in order to define precisely what a drone is and how law enforcement can and cannot use the technology as they pursue their mission. This law allows the use of drones only after obtaining a warrant, in pursuit of a terrorist threat when that threat has been determined by the United States Secretary of Homeland Security, or when a law enforcement agency has determined that "swift action" is needed to prevent the loss of life or serious property damage, and in the search for a missing person or persons (National Conference of State Legislatures 2013). Unique to this law is a very specific outline of the remedies that private persons may seek if they have been victim to inappropriate use of unmanned systems. Florida's law again does not limit access to the airspace, but limits the uses and applications of unmanned systems thereby maintaining the usefulness of the new technology, allowing law enforcement flexibility in their functions, and addressing the privacy concerns of their citizens.

Montana's SB 196 follows the same direction as Idaho and Florida, not limiting airspace access but limiting the manner by which information gained from UAS can be admitted as evidence in prosecution proceedings within the state. Again, the information can only be used if a search warrant has been granted and not as a manner to gain a search warrant (Montana State Legislature 2013). The law also excludes satellites in their definition of a "UAV" instead identifying them as "an aircraft that is operated without direct human intervention from on or within the aircraft." Tennessee published almost an identical piece of legislation ensuring compliance with search warrants, allowing the use of drones for counter-terrorist events, and allowing remedy for those that have been wronged by an invasion of privacy stemming from UAS usage.

Other states have acted beyond these three. While some do limit the role of UAS in their airspace, they have focused instead upon offering support to the industry through:

1. Explicit support of test center applications and funding for those test centers.
2. Clear and concise limitations that describe operational boundaries.

These two mechanisms identify the states as clear leaders in the competitive marketplace for the UAS industry. At the most supportive, Section 26 of North Dakota's SB 2018 granted "$1,000,000 from the state general fund" to pursue designation as an FAA UAS test site pledging an additional $4,000,000 in additional funds upon receiving the approval of the test center bid. In late 2013, North Dakota received one of six test site awards and are now fully operational as a test site facility. Hawaii's SB 1221 reflects the state's eagerness to pursue higher-education funding for unmanned systems by funding two staff positions at the University of Hawaii for the creation of degree and technical programs relating to advanced aviation—one of which must be a professional unmanned aircraft systems pilot program. Hawaii was a member of the Alaska test site bid and in late 2013 that team was granted a test site confirmation by the FAA.

The Texas state legislature recently enacted HB 912, illustrating how a state legislature can limit inappropriate uses of unmanned aircraft systems while supporting lawful and important law enforcement and commercial activities. In this legislation, Texas outlines 19 lawful uses of unmanned aircraft systems including their use in "airspace designated as an FAA test site, their use in connection with a valid search warrant, and their use in oil pipeline safety and rig protection" (National Conference of State Legislatures 2013). The act also creates two new Class-C misdemeanor crimes for the illegal use of an "image" attained from a UAS. The Department of Public Safety is also expected to report to the legislature on law enforcement agency use of UAS. The Texas legislature's balanced approach to UAS both supports growth of the UAS industry and provides limitations to law enforcement to allay fears over privacy. Texas A&M University at Corpus Christi was granted a test site in 2013.

The state most embracing of UAS activities nationwide is Alaska, and this surely played a role in their being selected for the first commercial authorization for UAS by the FAA. Alaska's HCR 6 is the nation's most supportive legislation through funding allocations, identification of positive unique qualities that define the UAS platform, and providing commercial access in deference to FAA decisions. This legislation clearly acknowledges the FAA's sole role in determining airspace access, while outlining why privacy is the concern of the state as "unmanned aircraft systems may present a substantial risk to privacy, but neither the Federal Aviation Administration nor any other state or federal agency currently has specific statutory authority to regulate privacy matters relating to unmanned aircraft systems." While acknowledging the privacy concerns that UAS may represent, and deferring throughout the bill text to the "Federal Aviation Administration . . . statutory authority," Alaska lauds the important positive qualities that define UAS as "designed for gathering information necessary to protect human life in search and rescue operations, aiding in the management of resources, including marine mammal and fisheries research." Alaska's legislation does not end there, where so many other states have simply limited use as a blanket theme without attempting to provide an outlet to grow the industry into something safe, secure, and lawful. As in the other supportive states, Alaska received approval as one of the six test sites for UAS by the FAA.

Alaska's HCR 6 puts together a meaningful and well-balanced "Task Force on Unmanned Aircraft Systems" to review the FAA regulations on drones and write recommendations and legislation that "protects privacy and allows [for] the use of unmanned aircraft system for public and private applications." It would be in the interest of Virginia, and many other states, to follow this example moving forward as it signals an appreciation for the unique qualities of UAS, acknowledges the statutory responsibilities and role of the FAA, and protects the interests of citizens concerned about privacy and looking to work in this innovative field. So far, Alaska has seen the first of a kind of commercial UAS certification for two different models—the Boeing Insitu Scan Eagle and the AeroVironment Puma AE—used for continuous glacial movement tracking, "man-over-board" search missions, mammal migration research, and oil field perimeter management. Working closely with the FAA, Alaska is enabling great commercial activity, important scientific research, and law enforcement gains that provide a role model for integration efforts nationwide.

Systems resist change. Those systems can be economic, political, mechanical, or macro-organic. It doesn't matter what type of system it is, they all require a catalyst and inputs to change their nature. Sometimes, the change is created naturally—as in erosion, changing opinions over time, or corrosive element introduction to a material. Other times we force change by an expanse of resources—a military coup, building a levy, or producing a vaccine. The first type of change requires time with few resources, and the other is expensive but can be done now. These changes for UAS are not gradual and the FAA is being hit by rapid, expansive change without the resources to deal with it. This system is changing and no one knows where it will end up.

While computers and automation have allowed significant gains in performance, they also created opportunities for hacking, have redefined the labor marketplace, and changed dramatically the way communication takes place. Unmanned aircraft do not represent the same level of threat to that status-quo, though the public and some legislators do see privacy as coming under attack. How the law protects privacy, how courts interpret that right to privacy and what makes the new technology uniquely qualified to offer a threat to that privacy must be well understood before stopping integration efforts or hindering law enforcement. The current situation varies by state— as noted above—however, one thing remains certain: the protection of civil society will only be improved with the use of remotely piloted aircraft.

Before understanding the challenges and rewards that UAVs offer, we must first understand how this new technology can impinge upon privacy or cause individuals to make the decision to illegally surveil. While unmanned aircraft make it easier, cheaper, and more effective to surveil a target—the case law developed over decades of privacy law cases require the same legal tests and arguments defining current aerial or ground-based evidence acquisition. This defines law enforcement's approach to unmanned aircraft systems. It is important for those concerned that UAS may hinder the ability of an individual to protect their privacy, to have a full understanding of the case law surrounding surveillance, reconnaissance, and search warrant execution.

Case study: The privacy dilemma – The Constitution and case law

Privacy concerns have been lumped in with UAS flights and government overreach in the United States for at least the last five years due to the conflation of reports of government spying and overreach, and the original nature of the drone technologies being military. In 2011, when quadcopters and other innovative developments were maturing to a point of commercialization, Julian Assange and Wikileaks began releasing secret US reports illustrating differences between what the public believed about overseas military operations in Afghanistan and Iraq, and what was really going on—highlighting the discrepancy between reality and government presentation to the public (Sanders and Downs 2011). Public distrust and the overreach of government entities became a major talking point in political discourse, impacting the rise of the Tea Party and other conservative elements in the United States, and slowing down the political support for UAS. In 2013, Edward Snowden began releasing secret reports and information on federal government programs using advanced technology-related tactics to spy on the American populace, again in previously unknown or underappreciated methods (Szoldra 2014). These two events, coinciding with presidential and local election rhetoric targeting technological spying and government overreach, spurred anti-drone feelings that are still felt today. This section highlights important principles, cases, and case law related to unmanned aircraft privacy concerns, protections, and information.

In the United States of America, the Fourth Amendment identifies protection from unlawful search and seizure and more recently has been understood by the Supreme Court to offer a right to privacy. Unlawful search and seizure requires any warrant to be sanctioned and supported by probable cause. Until now, the US Supreme Court has held that individuals do not generally have Fourth Amendment rights with respect to aerial surveillance because of "the ability that anyone might have to observe what could be viewed from the air." As it is easy to see a plane or helicopter directly overhead, or a camera mounted on a wall, you can reasonably understand your actions are under watch. As it is difficult to hide aerial surveillance, you don't have protection from it. Drones, though, can be small just as they can be very large. Drones can be easy to acquire, easy to fly, easy to maintain, and cheap to replace. Realizing that there are unique characteristics of this new technology—size, portability, low cost, ease of use—the case law surrounding privacy concerns and the use of new technologies may differ from previous case law. All current understanding of drone privacy cases seems to revolve upon whether or not there is a reasonable expectation of privacy or a physical attempt to create protection from surveillance from the air. The cases mentioned below all affect law enforcement's approach to UAS use and help outline state legislatures' limitations on UAS. The next few cases are not included chronologically but instead are based upon the element of privacy being discussed.

Katz v. United States (1967)

Katz is an illegal bookie. The FBI, knowing he is breaking federal law by taking wagers over the phone throughout the country, decides to wiretap the phone he is using for the wagers. They wiretap a phone booth that Katz frequently uses to take these wagers, and having recorded his phone calls, proceed to use the evidence to prosecute him. The Supreme Court found 7–1 that the FBI committed an unlawful search and seizure and violated Katz's Fourth Amendment rights even though the phone booth was in public—not in his home. If it had been in his home, there would be a reasonable assumption of privacy.

This case is crucial for UAS activity legality because the test employed to determine a constitutional violation—the Harlan Test—originated from this case. This test is used to determine if privacy protection is constitutionally afforded to the person in question and requires that:

1. A person must have an actual expectation for privacy.
2. That the expectation is reasonable.

This test frames the discussion of the case law moving forward and is vital in understanding that all protections of privacy are evaluated, in the eyes of the courts, by these two elements.

Kyllo v. United States (2001)

In *Kyllo v. United States*, law enforcement put to use a new technology not readily available to the public (thermal imager) to determine if Kyllo was breaking the law (growing 100 separate marijuana plants) in a garage. Without being granted a warrant, the Department of the Interior identified heat signatures emanating from the house that reflected an area where many lights were being used to accelerate the growth of the marijuana plants. Based on this evidence, the Department of the Interior obtained a search warrant and went on to arrest Danny Lee Kyllo. It is most important to note that the use of concerning technology (thermal imaging) came before the search warrant was granted.

The Supreme Court said that this use of advanced technology—because it was not readily available to the public (for cost, and availability)—was beyond the scope of what is allowable to law enforcement and constituted to some degree a search without warrant. This invalidated the use and application without search warrant and made law enforcement wary of advanced technology for surveillance. Law enforcement identifies the *Kyllo* case as the most significant limitation on UAS today. Often, sheriffs will have reasonable cause and perhaps could operate under the "swift action" clause of legal action for UAS, but they will refrain from using it for fear of having a case thrown out in prosecution (Frazier 2012). The understanding that because the technology is not readily available to the public, it is protected against, should be somewhat concerning to those privacy rights proponents. Recently, FLIR™ released a very affordable, roughly $250 handheld infrared camera adapter and application for smartphones. That same technology can be added to an unmanned aircraft with a gimbal for under $1,000. This, likely, will proliferate throughout the UAS commercial industry as infrared inspections are highly sought after. The question now becomes, what is the threshold for "accessibility" to the public and will that expectation of privacy change as drones are more frequent, advanced imaging systems become cheaper and proliferate, and how much will that protection of privacy invasion change based on this case.

Hester v. United States (1924)

Hester v. United States established the legal definition of "Curtilage," where privacy is considered to be protected in areas directly surrounding a domicile; the domicile being one place that is universally protected for privacy. The working definition of curtilage allows certain activities or objects to be afforded protection by the Fourth Amendment to some observers, but not all. Those areas that are defined as curtilage are adjacent to homes—backyards, fenced-in areas, etc. When properly hidden by a fence, or wall, or foliage these areas are offered Fourth Amendment protection from ground observers; however they are *not* afforded protection from air. Planes and helicopters that are flying are thought to be using public areas, and since a roof is not impeding their view from public airways, then they are considered viewable from a public area. They can be seen, goes the thought, by anyone from the general public who is flying.

While the previously discussed case, *Kyllo v. United States*, limits advanced or hard-to-acquire technologies, this has not traditionally afforded protection from helicopters and other flying platforms. These vehicles can be purchased and flown by the general public. What cannot be used is advanced imaging technologies such as infrared, night-vision, or chemo-signature lenses that are not readily available or could not reasonably be protected against.

Law enforcement officers have used aerial surveillance for a long time; employing commercial and non-commercial helicopters and fixed-wing aircraft with cameras. Throughout operations there have been significant court battles as to when illegal searches have been conducted from the air, the court siding with the law enforcement officers each time. In *California v. Ciraolo*, the Supreme Court ruled that the warrantless observation of a backyard does not violate the Fourth Amendment's protection against illegal search and seizure, and that though the yard may be shielded from view an airplane could take photographs above 1,000 feet (*California v. Ciraolo* 1986). In a similar case, the Supreme Court held in *Dow Chemical Co. v. United States* that though Dow Chemical clearly tried to keep the Environmental Protection Agency (EPA) from viewing their property when they requested a site-check, the EPA's hiring of a commercial aerial photographer using "precision aerial mapping camera" did not violate Dow Chemical's privacy rights (*Dow Chemical Co. v. United States* 1985). In *Florida v. Riley*, the Supreme Court found that Riley, the accused, did not have a reasonable expectation that his greenhouse—within which he was growing marijuana plants—was protected from aerial view, and thus helicopter surveillance did not qualify as a search under the Fourth Amendment (*Florida v. Riley* 1989). The finding directly affects the manner by which UAS operations are considered, for though the court did not say all aerial surveillance were legal, it did say, "any member of the public could legally have been flying over Riley's property in a helicopter at the altitude of 400 feet and could have observed Riley's Greenhouse. The Police officer did no more" (*Florida v. Riley* 1989). If the law enforcement agent is doing nothing more than a member of the public might, he is not in violation of the Fourth Amendment and thus able to operate any UAS as would another citizen. The question becomes, does UAS qualify as a new and advanced technology like the thermal imagers in *Kyllo* or do they qualify as helicopters as in *Riley* and *Ciraolo*? Once they become widely available to the public—it will be difficult to argue that it is a new and advanced technology from which a person could reasonably expect privacy. Therefore, a legislative approach that defines the "images" taken from a UAS, rather than a limitation of UAS for law enforcement, is the most reasonable if legislation is still to be pursued restricting their use.

While legislation surrounding UAS integration into the national airspace began with the passing of H.R. 658—FAA Modernization and Reform Act of 2012, tasking the FAA with the challenge of integrating UAS into the national airspace by 2015, the process has moved—as many in the industry believe—slowly. Those of us in the aviation safety world, better acquainted with the regulatory and standardization process, recognize the FAA movement forward takes time in order to create a framework that is inclusive of business and providing the safety that the public demands and requires.

Until recently, the FAA believed it had created guidance that would work as interim regulations which provided for a safe environment at home. Policy 8900.227 extensively outlined the process by which a pilot could fly in the national airspace, outlined the roles and responsibilities of those applying for flight plans, and outlined how the process for flying in the national airspace worked. While it wasn't perfect—and was extremely restrictive disallowing any forms of commercial endeavors by unmanned systems—the FAA was stalling for time productively as they developed standards to operate safely and securely amongst cooperative and non-cooperative aircraft. It wasn't until 2011 that a court decision—albeit from an NTSB administrative judge—determined that in fact these "internal documents" could not be considered regulation and therefore the FAA could not enforce their ban on commercial activities for small UAS.

Huerta v. Pirker (2011)

The story of *Huerta v. Pirker* began in 2011 when Raphael "Trappy" Pirker began flying his small, foam-sized unmanned aircraft above the cloud-free campus of Virginia Tech, in Charleston, Virginia. Trappy, a member of The Black Sheep R/C Club, had previously made it his responsibility to throw caution to the wind to capture, for commercial gain, aerial footage at low altitudes of locations all over the world. If you look online (specifically YouTube.com™) you will find a number of videos he and his team have put together committing what many consider very dangerous acts in the sky— flying over populated areas, landmarks, under and through high traffic areas like bridges and freeways, and claiming that they are in full control the whole time. It may be true that they are experts at what they do, and their systems are designed to higher specs than many other hobbyists. Ultimately, The Black Sheep Team had been trying to make waves for years, and finally in 2011, they caught the attention of the FAA.

After releasing the footage of their Virginia Tech flights soaring high above allowed altitude, within feet of historical monuments and under highway overpasses directly against traffic, Trappy was fined by the FAA $10,000 for "Careless or reckless operation of an aircraft" in violation of 14 CFR 91.13; "operating a commercial drone in an unsafe manner." In response, having received just the result Black Sheep was looking for from the FAA, Pirker moved to dismiss the charges immediately on the grounds that Federal Aviation Regulations do not apply to model aircraft flight operations. He also asserted in the response that the FAA never published an applicable regulation using the required NPRM (Notice of Proposed Rule Making). Strictly speaking, he was right on both accounts. The FAA never used the NPRM process— in violation of the Administrative Procedures Act—and therefore could not be seen to have a regulation on the books by which to enforce. What the FAA was enforcing was an Advisory Circular—AC 91-57 (Federal Aviation Administration AAT-220 1981). This Advisory Circular had added certain restrictions to hobbyist flights which traditionally allowed remote control pilots the ability to fly their aircraft in specific locations and for specific purposes. AC 91-57 had stipulated certain operating standards that would enable certain aircraft to fly, and therefore had intentionally separated out remote control aircraft from manned aircraft. Passed in 1981, however, it did not take into consideration the new technological developments that enable unmanned aircraft to proliferate. The restrictions delineated in AC 91-57 were:

- An operation site away from populated areas.
- No spectators when aircraft is not proven airworthy.
- No higher than 400ft AGL.
- Give right of way to manned aircraft.
- Do not fly within three miles of an airport without permission.

The FAA's response to Pirker's appeal was that the statutory definition of "aircraft" must incorporate any device intended for flight—including model aircraft—and therefore Pirker should be subject to other FAA regulations; namely 14 CFR 91.13—the original statute the FAA had said was in violation. They said that operators of commercial drones are subject to FAA policy statements governing model aircraft operations, AC 91-57, which stated that "operators who wish to fly an unmanned aircraft for civil use must obtain an FAA airworthiness certificate the same as any other type of aircraft."

The judge ruled in favor of Mr Pirker, noting that there was no enforceable FAA rule applicable to model aircraft under which the FAA could assess fines, and that because the FAA had historically distinguished between unmanned commercial devices from other "aircraft"—by modifying that term with the prefix "model"—the regulations could not apply to model aircraft (National Transportation Safety Board 2014). Finally, the judge admonished the FAA for trying to skirt their regulatory responsibility, and identified that the FAA's other policy statements used in assessing unmanned aircraft operations for commercial use are non-binding, because the agency issued the statements as internal documents, never subjecting them to the NPRM process. At this point, the following was made clear:

- AC 91-57 is voluntary.
- FAA's reliance on AC 91-57 is invalid as it is clarified later that AC 91-57 "specifically excludes individuals or companies from flying model aircraft for business purposes."

What was made most clear at this point was that the FAA would appeal, as seemingly the floodgates were open and the FAA had no power to regulate any unmanned aircraft system. The FAA did appeal to the full NTSB. The determination by the Board was that the FAA "does have the power to regulate unmanned aircraft systems" as UAS are considered aircraft. The FAA has been empowered by Congress to regulate aircraft, and the civil penalty imposed by the FAA for operating an aircraft in a careless manner is legal and within the jurisdiction of the FAA. While this decision was lamented by much of the sUAS community, those more reasonable voices understood that for the autonomous aircraft industry to flourish, working with the FAA and not at odds with the FAA under reasonable and fair, published, regulations would be the best step forward. Thus, the *Huerta v. Pirker* case had probably the greatest impact on the developing industry by pressuring the FAA to publish the sUAS regulations quickly and inclusive of the greater drone community.

Lessons learned from relevant cases

Are drones an entirely new phenomenon or are they just a better, more efficient version of aerial photography? The case law that exists from aerial surveillance via manned aircraft still applies until unmanned aviation has a more recent precedent and there isn't much of a difference between a manned and unmanned aircraft. The courts have generally stymied the use of surveillance techniques upon the general public where there is a reasonable expectation of privacy. The greatest concern for those who value privacy the most, wonder when the proliferation of new technologies begins to diminish the expectation of privacy and how or when will the courts decide that because the technologies are accessible enough, the privacy that a backyard afforded against a small drone doesn't exist any longer.

Those seeking to ban drones in general airways must understand that the entirety of what drones do is make it smaller, quieter, and more cost-effective to execute the same mission that law enforcement already conduct. The technology isn't much different than a small helicopter or plane with a camera on it, the locations haven't changed from previous cases, and ultimately the courts won't differ from previous precedents. While the differences between manned and unmanned craft matter, this is not a new problematic technology to be outlawed, but an opportunity to define the current legal guidelines of aviation surveillance for mutual growth and inclusion.

The PATRIOT Act, Title I—Title X, enhanced significantly the authority of law enforcement and intelligence agencies and went unchecked until 2012 when H.R. 5925 was introduced in order to rein in the overreaching, privacy violating groups that Congress believed to be violating the Constitution through the use of unmanned aircraft systems. The House of Representatives acted by including in this resolution the following:

> To protect individual privacy against unwarranted governmental intrusion through the use of unmanned aerial vehicles commonly called drones and for other purposes . . .

Section 2
. . . shall not use a drone to gather evidence or other information pertaining to criminal conduct . . . except to the extent authorized in a warrant issued

Great efforts were brought forth on the part of the sheriffs, police, Customs and Border Protection, National Guard, Coast Guard and many other law enforcement organizations who felt strongly that this legislation actually went beyond how other technologies are regulated.

H.R. 6199—Preserving American Privacy Act of 2012—was introduced and it also was defeated. This resolution stated that:

> drones could not be used domestically by law enforcement for surveillance of a U.S. national except pursuant to a warrant and in the investigation of felony.

This legislation would have put more restrictions into effect limiting only law enforcement's ability to use *surveillance and reconnaissance* attained by unmanned aircraft systems; the resolution ended for lack of support.

Thus far, the federal government has not been able to come to a consensus on how far privacy concerns need to be protected; the question being asked is whether or not there is a functional difference between manned and unmanned aircraft surveillance tools. The justice system seems to treat them as the same. Law enforcement, acting under this assumption, though with deference to underutilizing this technology for fear of nullifying arrests, have therefore been hesitant to incorporate UAS into their everyday operations. What law enforcement is calling for across the nation is appropriate and distinct guidelines as to when they can and cannot use this very important, potentially life-saving tool in the pursuit of suspects. As of now, law enforcement operates under the assumption that this tool can be utilized much like manned aviation and used under the same restrictions that have become precedent through case law.

What is of even greater concern is not the extent to which law enforcement is permitted to use unmanned aircraft, but the extent to which privacy can be protected against private individuals. While covered in previous sections it is worth reiterating that the private use of unmanned aircraft is a much greater danger to the average person. Those who can unbox a flying 4k resolution camera and begin filming over their neighbor's backyard with few ramifications without further legislative protections at the state level (if necessary) should worry the population much more than government invasion.[9]

8 Developing a community

The UAS operators, policy makers, manufacturers, educators, and public at large are very disconnected and yearning for relationships that help some feel safe, others motivated to help, and of course some better equipped to make money. In lieu of meaningful and rich relationships that have evolved over the last century as manned aviation has, unmanned aviation seems to be lost in a sea of uncertainty and is being ravaged by predatory wolves all looking to make a buck without adding value to the discussion. A variety of organizations exist that are positive players in the UAS environment; however, even those have elements within them that seek to promote only their interests at the cost of the well-being of the UAS community. The Association for Unmanned Vehicle Systems International (AUVSI), acting as the largest and most robust advocacy group for commercial and defense unmanned systems, is often mired in internal strife with member chapters from the East Coast seeking to have greater connection with FAA and DoD activities, while on the West Coast virulent voices call for the condemnation and breaking of ties from the FAA. AUVSI of course is not the only community member that matters, and so this chapter will focus on the resources and stakeholders that any UAS enthusiast, pilot, or manufacturer would do well to know and become active in.

The specter of government oversight and involvement often scares all but the most seasoned UAS veterans. However, those with experience in the field and a good understanding of the role of government in providing a safe environment for flight, recognize that reaching out to air traffic control, FAA, law enforcement, or emergency crews can only help your operation. Do not think of the government as the bogeymen trying to stop your fun, your mission, or your payday. They are people too, they want to see the industry succeed and part of that is enabling safe and secure operations for UAS. What is also important to note is that just because the likelihood of your being caught acting inappropriately is slim in most cases, and the protection of anonymity that UAS provides is vast, increasingly the FAA is seeking innovative ways to regulate the industry and to provide the enforcement requisite to ensure a safe national airspace.

Stakeholders in the integration space on the government side range from those overseeing the newest technology developments, like NASA, to law

Figure 8.1 Awaiting Flight. Lone UAV awaiting a military mission in
         a hanger © Digital Storm

enforcement entities like the Federal Bureau of Investigation, Airborne Law
Enforcement Association (ALEA), local municipal governments and state
government legislators. This book has outlined many of the outcomes and
participation of these entities, and so we won't elaborate again here; however
the need for involvement from regulators, legislators, and enforcement drive
a need for all members to understand the roles the others play. Practicing
interactions with law enforcement in the case of incident, accident, or simple
questioning is a very important exercise that all flight operators should
undertake, just like interacting with the public or media outlets.

The communities discussed basically breakdown into three categories that
will all be recognized with examples for each:

1. Advocacy and membership groups.
2. Educational entities.
3. Manufacturers, vendors, and companies.

Advocacy and membership groups

The Association for Unmanned Vehicle Systems International (AUVSI) is
among the most advanced, sophisticated, well-established, and politically savvy
groups in the unmanned field. They have hosted annual conferences for

decades and seek to advocate through education. Their motto, "advancing the unmanned systems and robotics community through education, advocacy and leadership," highlights the main facets of their mission, though even that message has had to change as technology develops and markets mature. They seek to bring in to the fold as many college and high school students as possible through their Robot Academy, University Programs, and recruiting mechanisms while maintaining lasting government relationships. At the state level, AUVSI requires individuals to begin chapters for the advocacy organization based around local members and their interests. These chapters are numerous throughout the United States and act on behalf of the national chapter as liaison to groups, fundraising, and member outreach. If you're interested, you can see the growing list of AUVSI chapters at the following link: http://www.auvsi. org/membershipandchapters/chapters.

AUVSI has been a world leader in commercially focused research and helped re-focus the discussion from privacy concerns to regulatory matters during a time when drones were synonymous with murder, spying, and government overreach. At the time their membership—heavily rooted in DoD relationships—had split along ideological lines. Where some members who had extensive experience, knowledge, and investment with the Department of Homeland Security and Department of Defense would rather have seen regulations develop through a more regulated, constrictive, and safety-focused manner, other members focused on the hobby and civil commercial industry, looking for AUVSI to act as a lobbying group seeking less restrictive, faster regulation publication. While both interests do overlap to some degree, it is a very difficult tightrope that outgoing AUVSI President Michael Toscano and Executive Vice-President Gretchen West had to walk as calls from both sides grew louder.

In 2014, on the heels of the Pirker Decision at Virginia Tech and as the FAA regulatory frameworks continued to stale lacking a promised NPRM, voices within AUVSI and external to it began seeking new venues for investment. Countless new conferences were popping up all over the United States and abroad, and competition grew dramatically. New organizations, focused on making profits through major conferences, specific to commercial initiatives such as InterDrone or the Commercial Drone Expo, arose seeking to capitalize on the blossoming commercial industry. Among other advocacy groups, Unmanned Systems Technology, the sUAS Expo in San Francisco, and the AUVSA International Drone Expo—clearly attempting to leverage the success of AUVSI for their own interests—became available to provide outlets for face to face discussion though largely less impressive than AUVSI.

Perhaps one of the more vocal and proactively anti-government regulations entities is sUAS News and its leadership. This group, while very informative and a great resource for the latest in drone news, also comes with the bias normally expected in cable news. Podcasts associated with many of these membership groups also provide insight into the approach to UAS technology.

Figure 8.2 AUVSI XPONENTIAL conference sign at New Orleans, Louisiana 2016

The American Modelers Association (AMA) is also a group that seeks to help build the development, education, and training of amateur and professional modelers through civic engagement, online forums, and membership events. The AMA self-identifies as a group that fosters young amateur aviation enthusiasts through modeling and flight of remote control aeronautics. They publish a magazine entitled *Model Aviation* quarterly that can be subscribed to via their website www.modelaircraft.org. AMA members have seen the development of unmanned aircraft systems as a double-edged sword for their interests as it has expanded news and discussion surrounding their hobby in remote flight tremendously, but taken over much of the discussion with easy-to-fly systems that take little training. Estimations for the size of modeling prior to the miniaturization of internal flight controllers and GPS enabling capabilities for flight data management were showing the sport of model aircraft diminishing consistently prior to sUAS promulgation. The AMA is somewhat torn, it seems, with how to approach sUAS. In a discussion at AUVSI with the President of the AMA, he acknowledged that some AMA club fields do not treat sUAS pilots with the same respect and acknowledgment as many of the other aircraft. He did, however, acknowledge that for the AMA to survive, young and innovative new members would be needed to "foster change from within" and to help develop that appreciation for quadcopters.

There are a number of opportunities for students to be involved with the AMA and they incentivize this involvement through the "Take-off and Grow (TGA) Grant Program," free radio control flight instruction, and model aviation student clubs that offer reduced price and free memberships for students pursuing the hobby of model aviation. If you are a student in high school or college and looking to fly unmanned aircraft in the future, I strongly encourage you to be involved with the AMA, and learn through the community-based safety standards they have developed.

Many organizational groups such as the AMA, the Remotely Controlled Pilots Association, and drone racing clubs throughout the United States have gone on record of being frustrated with the FAA's reluctance to recognize their sUAS expertise and guidance as the fundamental form of safety regulations (Remote Control Aerial Platform Association 2014). They believe that decades of modeling experience and lack of major accidents reflect an opportunity to provide leadership in the new industry. FAA, alternatively, has increasingly acted to forego these community-based standards as the measure for model aircraft safety, instead choosing to codify standards through the industry-based approach of ASTM and RTCA domestically, and with deference to the JARUS, EUROCAE in Europe, and ICAO more generally. There are many people who have spent nearly a decade working through these industry consensus groups who are also figureheads and members of the RCAPA and AMA efforts, so these groups are not mutually exclusive and often have very similar discussions and problems that are addressed.

Educational entities

Perhaps the most worrisome entities that are arising all over the world purport to outline the important facets of education and offer pilot certifications without any form of accreditation, or concrete knowledge of how certification will work. These entities are not affiliated with a Part 61 educational operation, nor a four-year university or two-year college program, are specifically focused on only unmanned training, and cannot support their claims that their credential, program certificate, or training will certify the student for any sort of regulation or indemnification of duties. These groups generally host ex-military members as "Deans" or "Directors" and then shop out the educational material and presentations to model aircraft enthusiasts, those who have been operating illegally for a few years, or who can showcase aerial images that are impressive. What is fundamental to understand is that at the moment of writing, there exists no unmanned aircraft specific licensing program certified by the Federal Aviation Administration in the United States.

These educational entities have been in operation for quite some time, following the increased interest in unmanned aircraft. Prior to the latest 14 CFR 107 publication, a private pilot's license or sports pilot license was the lowest barrier to entry for accreditation of skill for unmanned flight. With the sUAS Final Rule, a separate remote pilot certification was created to help provide an outlet for all those interested in pursuing sUAS flight under very specific conditions. This certification, at least under 14 CFR 107, requires the passing of an aeronautical knowledge test administered at a certified FAA test center. While of course the knowledge contained on the tests may be taught, only the FAA designated test centers may certify the accreditation. There are already schools catering to the teaching of this information, but largely, the general knowledge can be attained through the existing online pilot training materials available online or at Part 61 flight schools.

Conversely, a number of very good, very advanced, and important research and training institutions have set themselves apart from the rest as they continue to offer certifications for maintenance, unmanned systems management, flight operations, safety and security training, and air traffic management within the context of unmanned systems. Among these very high-quality institutions in the United States are University of North Dakota, Kansas State University, Virginia Polytechnic State University, Embry-Riddle University, and the University of Southern California's Aviation Safety and Security Program. Each of these programs represents world leadership in their particular training focus—for example, USC is the world leader in training for safety professionals looking to lead unmanned systems operations in their unique course entitled Safety Management Systems for Remotely Piloted Aircraft.[10] University of North Dakota provides education coupled with the opportunity to engage in the test site at Northern Plains, North Dakota, situated close by their main campus as does Virginia Tech as the lead member of the Mid-Atlantic Aviation Partnership. These major institutions continue to contribute enormously to the standards development and data testing efforts that shape the future of UAS today. From their safety information and provision of internally developed checklists, to materials analysis and failure rate information, they provide meaningful research to commercial operations since inception.

What is most important in looking at the educational environment when pursuing a certification or degree is who recognizes that university or program as an expert, and will it help with finding a position you are looking for. Also, the facilities within which education will take place are vital to understanding the capabilities of the organization and the interactive missions that will be considered. Previous to 2016, if an organization had no Certificate of Authorization or Waiver, there may have been no flights included in your training, or the simulation of missions may have been insignificant or minimal.

In an announcement in 2016, the FAA outlined efforts to enable students to fly sUAS in support of research without strenuous approvals in the interest of educational efficacy. The outcome of this change has yet to have a major impact, but in combination with 14 CFR 107, ramifications are likely to provide a proliferation of student research and data. Understanding the partnerships that a training organization is party to is a very important way to understand how an organization perceives its role in the UAS industry.

The final training participants that should be mentioned are the roles of consulting companies like Wolf UAS LLC, MITRE, and MTSI. These groups often provide leading safety and management advice to developing programs lacking the overall knowledge of important program needs. When seeking out help for developing a program, it is vital that you research the organization providing training to determine their place in the industry. Look for whom the consulting company is partnered with, which stakeholders have found their use valuable and important, and determine how many field operations experience or successful missions they have been a party to.

Manufacturers, vendors, and companies

It would be impossible to create a comprehensive list of all manufacturers, vendors, or companies that are impacting the development of UAS. From the big to the small, innovators in the fields of supply chain management, software, hardware, and integration have a tremendous role in the direction the industry is taking. As discussed, many of the companies fall into two categories—small hardware/software companies focusing on the small UAS industry markets such as the small commercial drones, anti-drone technologies, and sensor platforms that are little more than flying cameras. The second group consists of large companies with the internal support to take a chance on "pie in the sky" ideas.

The small start-up, innovation-oriented, low-resource, high-impact companies are finding consolidation and investment through VC and technology acquisition. DroneDeploy, SkyCatch, 3D Robotics, DJI, Parrot, Yuneec, and SenseFly™ are all good examples of the traditional "new company" model that looks for investments, develops hardware or software to meet certain market needs, and finds success in the market place. Of course, DJI (the Chinese mega company now leading in all facets of the sUAS industry) started as a unique leader in the drone field from very early on and truly became the first user-focused experience. By promoting user-interface, easy flight, and a combination of capabilities that had previously required piecemeal building, they revolutionized the approach to UAS sales. 3D Robotics competed with them for a number of years; however, recognizing they had been beaten on the hardware front, they decided to focus on excelling through software and education.

Many small companies are finding success in the software integration and platform development with a system agnostic approach. By creating a platform or better software installation that can work on any drone hardware solution, they open themselves up to a larger customer base. By adopting the DJI API, they allow their "better" software to find a home on the leading platforms. Software companies such as Airmap, Drone Deploy, and Drone Log Book are great examples of how a software company can find success through adoption of many platforms.

The second type of company are the larger, corporate entrepreneurs who have found success in adopting drone platforms for their organizations, thereby driving innovation through decision-making rather than creation. Aerovironment, Boeing Insitu, and Lockheed Martin are classical players in the field of UAS and helped drive the formation and standardization, even success of the industry, through constant development and defense-funded budgetary cycles. More recently, they have all taken a focus on delving into the commercial drone space. Boeing Insitu's ScanEagle and Aerovironment's Puma AE both led the charge as the first commercial drones authorized through the Special Airworthiness Certification in Alaska, and both have found great success as pipeline monitors, wildlife migration trackers, and various other operations. However, these larger platforms are not the only focus of major companies. Unlike the start-up companies finding innovative success in this new commercial market, corporate entrepreneurship by Airbus, BNSF Railroad, Qualcomm, Intel, Amazon, UPS, DHL, and GoPro have all driven the discussion, media attention, and investment into drones. Amazon is of course testing package delivery in the United States and the United Kingdom, as is DHL in Germany, while UPS continues to discuss such plans. BNSF Railroad led a pilot project with the Mid-Atlantic Aviation Partnership to identify capabilities and shortcomings in railroad monitoring by sUAS, in the hopes that their railroad tracks could be monitored continuously from the air. Qualcomm and Intel continues to invest in technology accelerators producing autonomous vehicles and software that utilize their chipsets, communication systems, and collaborate with the rest of the investment portfolios. Google X, the moonshot factory, is also one of the most important players in the drone marketplace as they are developing three types of unique, forward-thinking projects all focused on automated flight: Project Loon, Project Wing, and Project Makani. These three platforms, in conjunction with the announcement of developing a $100 ADS-B system, could revolutionize the way Internet is delivered, packages are delivered, and energy is gathered.

Finally, there are a number of safety-oriented organizations that are beginning to provide the certification, inspections, audits, and training requisite for this newly flourishing industry. ISBAO/IBAC, Wyllis, Wyvern, and other certification groups provide the needed expertise for external inspections and audits that provide meaningful feedback for organizations open to third-party support. These vendors serve a vital role in the development and continuous promotion of SMS for organizations and will be essential in the near and long term though their necessity is little recognized by many of the smaller drone companies currently. Wolf UAS, the author's company, provides this type of support for documentation and analysis of programmatic difficulties through a variety of

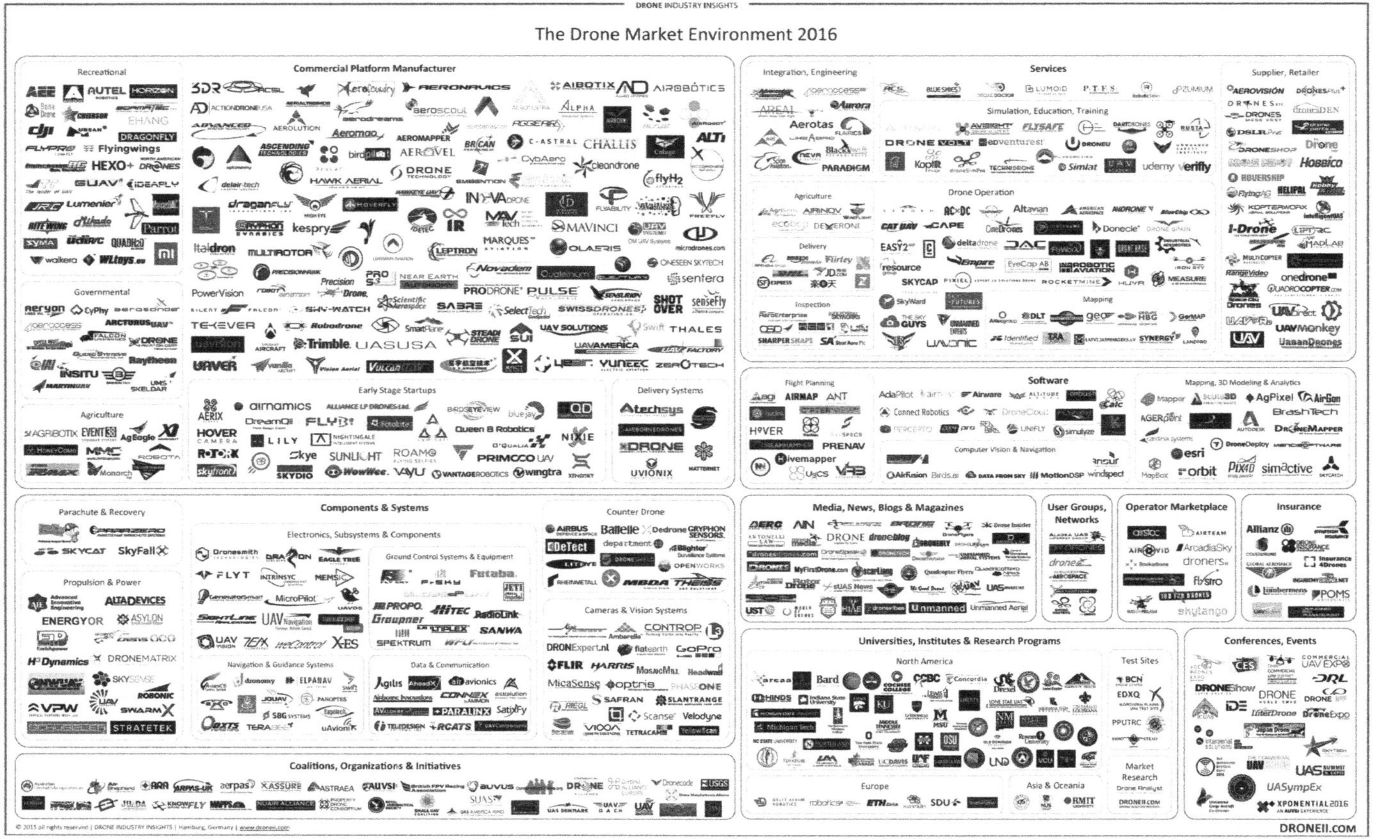

Figure 8.3 Industry map put together by Droneii.com

organizational analysis tools developed in the world of aviation and applied to unmanned aviation. Among these are onsite audits, Information Systems Analysis, Quality Management System development, and performance review or interview of employees and contractors. Meanwhile, many contractors and consultants can provide the training and insights needed to bring an organization into compliance with regulatory requirements, or into conformity and compliance with SMS theory and ICAO/FAA safety thought leadership.

While this is certainly not a comprehensive list, the movers and shakers in the drone industry provide an amorphous market profile that provides new entrants access to investment, and yet also provides a very competitive environment for company success. These companies are driving the direction of the market, are all heavily involved in the standards and regulation development through proxy lobbyist groups such as Hogan Lovells, the Small UAV Coalition, the Commercial Drone Alliance, and less visible organizations.

One message may not fit all: An interview with Gretchen West

The unmanned systems industry is characterized by motivated, passionate, and visionary leaders who can appreciate many facets of the complex technologies evolving every day. Gretchen West is one of those leaders who has been involved in the unmanned aircraft community from its infancy, having acted as the Executive Vice-President for AUVSI, in conjunction with other roles, from October 2004 to 2014, going on to become the Vice-President of Business Development and Regulatory Affairs for a major commercial UAS company Drone Deploy, the Senior Advisor for Innovation and Technology with a world-leading policy and legal firm Hogan Lovells US LLP, and most recently co-founder and co-Executive Director of a professional association for commercial drone pilots, the Commercial Drone Alliance.

Though she is clearly a leader in the field of UAS now, she began her career in a manner similar to so much of the homegrown UAS industry—by learning the ins and outs of the military, hobbyist, and commercial drone operations without much previous experience in remote control aviation specifically, or aviation more generally. Ms. West is also one of very few women executives in the UAS field, most often dominated by male executives from the military sector. She continues to help push the boundaries for women innovators throughout robotics, exemplified in her continued role as a Discussion Leader for Women in Robotics with AUVSI in 2016.

As Gretchen West tells it, the future of unmanned systems has evolved rapidly and with many turns over the past 25 years, and her appreciation for the different characteristics of these systems has grown. As an executive manager in the UAS field for a major advisory and lobbying association (AUVSI), a private commercial company (Drone Deploy), and a Silicon Valley-based professional association (the Commercial Drone Alliance), her thoughts on the UAS industry direction are highly sought by industry participants, stakeholders, and investors all looking for success in this nascent market place. She has become a major force in where UAS investment and innovation heads, providing much needed wisdom and guidance to fledgling drone companies, end-users, technology experts, and legislators.

Though she serves on the advisory Board for Skyward, Nightingale Intelligent Systems, and Aerobo you can tell when you speak with her that her interests in this field come from a passion for technology development in its purest form, and for the prosperity and good of all people that the UAS industry can accomplish.

Gretchen is not alone in how she came to the UAS industry. Before finding herself leading the most important advocacy efforts and helping to envision the future of UAS regulations, her background was focused in non-profit management. She originally came into AUVSI as the seventh hire, meaning she was there from a very early stage and helped to build the largest UAS drone conference and advocacy membership group in the world. Her role there had focused on business development, where she "fell in love with the community and even today sees it as a tight knit group of people, working together to be committed to safety and reliability." She explains that a crossroads for AUVSI came when a new CEO was installed, and as part of that appointment she was kept on at the company to become the Executive Vice-President. Back then, AUVSI was focused on providing military customers with private suppliers and for all groups to advertise their latest systems. From humble beginnings in 1972, originally established as the National Association of Remotely Piloted Vehicles (NARPV), AUVSI grew into a nationally recognized leader in all facets of unmanned vehicles; renamed the Association for Unmanned Vehicle Systems International (AUVSI) in 1978.

The role of AUVSI began changing during Ms. West's oversight, when she led the charge for change. She recognized early on that as the industry got more popular, bigger, and more mainstream it would begin to see competition from other drone conferences, associations, and alliances that focused on very specific issues. Though other conferences were being established, there were no other providers of a magazine, tradeshow, foundation, and membership support that offered anywhere near the level of interaction, advocacy, or education that AUVSI could provide. As time went on, and much to do with the quickly developing push for commercial UAS, representation and advocacy efforts began to include relationships with law enforcement and then commercial UAS entities. As the membership grew, questions began to arise that AUVSI still faces today. For an advocacy organization with such dissimilar members, "How do you have a singular message?" When half your members are interested in regulation, oversight, vendors, or products for high-altitude hellfire missile carrying drones and the other half interested in low-altitude commercial drones, how do you provide a single marketplace of ideas and advocacy that provide equal resources and attention? These questions are still faced by AUVSI today and many other groups operating in the UAS space. Some are answering these questions better than others.

The Small UAV Coalition, of which Gretchen West was also an Advisor and served on the Board of Directors for, may have suffered from a similar issue—trying to represent both commercial and end-users. The one message, as she says, really doesn't work for both interests, which led to Ms. West's development of the Commercial Drone Alliance working to serve only end-users in the UAS field. This is not an environment catering to everyone, which may be exactly why it succeeds where so many other institutions have failed; by not trying to be too much to everyone. By providing an environment for specific users to gain insights and help from like-minded operators, the room won't be cluttered with noise as so often is the case in less focused organizations.

The hobbyist and commercial divide is another important collision of interests that Ms. West has a lot of experience handling through her time in the UAS industry, and one that doesn't receive much attention. Many commercial operators understand that the hobbyist community doesn't want to be overregulated. With significant push from the modeler community, there will be a tendency to provide regulatory provisions that lower the bar of responsibility for many operations. Commercial operators, and safety experts, feel as though regulation done correctly will help keep the skies operating safely—something much needed for the long-term success of the UAS industry. Conflict exists where the commercial operators are concerned that the lowest common denominator will be allowed to impinge on their market, driving down protections until an incident or accident culminates in public reputation loss, or even an elimination of commercial operations.

In balancing these fears and managing both communities, she says that traditionally you have modelers who have followed AMA community guidelines that have kept radio frequencies separated, right-of-way rules understood, and safety training to an acceptable level to keep everyone happy at specific airfields. On the other hand, she says, you have military unmanned aviation that was governed by themselves: both communities operating in separate worlds. AUVSI began getting involved a long time ago, warning about commercialization. Though these are still both separated worlds, now you have those who want to integrate beyond these easily separated and controlled environments. Real Estate photographers, Videographers, and inspectors—the consumer, prosumer, commercial. These are people who simply want to check their roof after a hailstorm, or take pictures of damage for insurance. These are the farmers wanting to fly a drone, or people flying in their backyard. They are not a community. In the past everyone had aeronautical knowledge like airspace or some rules. Most people today don't even know we're discussing airspace issues, they just want to fly safely and have a good time.

It's hard not to agree 100 per cent when you're talking with Gretchen West as she discusses with passion and dynamism the future of UAS. End-users, she says, are the most underrepresented people in the drone community and it's fairly easy to see why. Public perception, she says, is a very big deal and for a long time press-coverage of drones has all been negative. There are not enough individuals on the Hill, she says, that are friendly to drones and

UAS—a major hurdle to overcome. "We, the Commercial Drone Alliance," she points out, "want to highlight how cellular companies lose four men per year falling off ladders, but now they do that job using drones for inspection."

Another example is BNSF railway, which is part of the FAA pathfinder mission for rail inspections and very close to ending that program. While the support on the Hill exists for railway inspections using drones, this type of operation needs beyond visual line of sight capabilities. While there is a rule making for flying closer to people scheduled to be announced sometime in fall 2016, there is no word yet on the potential timeline for BVLOS operations. If it doesn't come soon, BNSF may have to pull the plug. They would go from wanting to invest in an "air force of drones" to nothing if the regulations don't allow the business plan to succeed. This is why advocacy and policy are so important.

Ms. West believes the future of UAS is bright. She reminds everyone that the industry is moving at a much better, quicker, more adapting pace than it had. "We went from 8 to 10 years for the first rulemaking to be finalized, and now we have another coming out in about a year." One to two years is still too long, she says, but it's certainly a step in the right direction and a trend that will hopefully continue. Another important consideration, she acknowledges, is that the FAA may be moving toward industry consensus standards. These industry consensus standards would allow major players to come together with the FAA to create the regulatory framework that governs technology adoption and performance metrics and it is clearly pointed out in Advisory Circular 107, published alongside 14 CFR 107, that the FAA is open to that approach. To her, the question will be, "Can industry come together to develop standards?" She thinks it may be good news for moving rapidly, but there may be major problems with that as well.

Finally, Gretchen West leaves off with a reminder that unmanned aircraft systems are tools to be used safely, and in support of a mission. The technologies that will affect the safety and regulators matter. The sweet spot for success, to her, is in developing new ways for newly acquired data to be used and understood. There is already great technology to acquire data, but if that data can't be easily understood or integrated, then it really has little or no use. The best example might be once again the farmers. Farmers don't really care about the drone itself, but care about the data and how it will help increase their crop, diminish their use of chemicals, or help diminish their impact on the environment. Whether that image is from a satellite or a drone, it doesn't really matter.

Notes

1 NextGen is a huge topic beyond the scope of this book. Suffice it to say that the NextGen is the FAA's most robust and complete overhaul of the aging national air space system incorporating new technologies like GPS, auto-configuration models, and plane-to-plane terminal collision avoidance systems in an effort to reduce fuel consumption, increase passenger loads, reduce noise pollution, and promote safety. NextGen will affect all aviation throughout domestic and international aviation.

2 The hot air balloon on a tether or even kites have been assimilated into the unmanned aircraft story, but really the unmanned aircraft story tends to develop just within the last 60 years or so.

3 A private association organized by agricultural unmanned helicopter pilots for evaluation and certifying the qualifications of agricultural unmanned helicopter pilots since there are no provisions for the qualifications in the current Aviation Act in Korea.

4 At the time of the accident.

5 This topic will be expanded on when discussing court cases. For now, it is important to understand that the FAA had not published regulatory guidance beyond Advisory Circular AC 91-57 outlining hobby and non-hobby use of unmanned aircraft and policy memos. It wouldn't be until the *Pirker v. Huerta* Case that the FAA would be definitively said to have jurisdiction over commercial UAS.

6 An NPRM is the state of a rule as it is being shown to the public and released for public comment. This form of the final rule takes into consideration all comments put forth during the comment phase and therefore the sUAS NPRM may have further changes prior to its publication (expected July 2016).

7 The author of this book had the privilege of serving on the RTCA SC-203 Human Factors Workgroup, and currently serves on the ASTM F-38.02 Subcommittee Workgroup focused on operational risk assessment. SC-203 was sunsetted, and now RTCA SC 228 has taken over much of the work effort in RTCA regarding large UAS.

8 These are both products (hardware and software) developed by SenseFly™ and for specific integration into that platform.

9 It should also be noted that as time goes on more and more case law regarding unmanned aircraft systems and their operations will expand the legal understanding of drone use. Identifying key leaders in the field is fundamentally important to developing your understanding of drone law. There are a number of leaders in the field, and this chapter should not be considered as legal advice. For specific legal advice seek the advice of an attorney specializing in UAS law.

10 The author may be somewhat biased as he created and teaches this course at the University of Southern California.

Bibliography

Ackerman, Spencer. 2013. *Drone Boosters, Not Cops, are the Biggest US Robot Market*. February 5. Accessed March 18, 2016. http://www.wired.com/2013/02/drone-farm/.

ASTM F-38.02 Work Group. 2016. *WK49619 Standard Practice/Guide for Operational Risk Assessment of Small Unmanned Aircraft Systems (UAS)*. Draft Standard, Version 3, ASTM.

Austro Control: AOT and LSA. 2014. *Airworthiness and Operational Notice Nr. 67*. Operational Notice for Unmanned Aircraft up to 150kg, Austria: Austro Control.

California v. Ciraolo. 1986. 476 U.S. 207 (1986) (U.S. Supreme Court, May 19).

Charles Katz v. United States. 1967. 389 U.S. 347 (1967) (U.S. Supreme Court, December 18).

Congressional Business Office. 2013. *The Budget and Economic Outlook: Fiscal Years 2013 to 2023*. February 2013. https://www.cbo.gov/publication/43907/.

Dana, Bill. 1973. *F-15 Drone Flight Report, Flight Number D-4-6*. National Aeronautics and Space Administration DFRC. Edwards, CA.

Davis, Rodney. 2016. Amendment to H.R. 4441. February 8, 2016. http://transportation.house.gov/uploadedfiles/daviro_038_xml.pdf/.

Dekker, Sydney. 2006. *The Field Guide to Understanding Human Error*. Aldershot: Ashgate.

Deloitte. 2012. *The Aerospace and Defense Industry in the U.S. A Financial and Economic Impact Study*. Global, March.

Dow Chemical Co. v. United States. 1985. 476 US 227 (1986) (U.S. Supreme Court, December 10).

Durkee, Matthew. 2007. *Highbeam Research*. August 26. Accessed March 1, 2014. https://www.highbeam.com/doc/1G1-168033281.html/.

Ehrhard, Thomas. *Air Force UAVs: The Secret History*. A Mitchell Institute Study. July 2010. file:///C:/Users/Wolf%20UAS%20LLC/Desktop/ADA525674.pdf/.

Elias, B., C. Brass, and R. Kirk. 2013. *Sequestration at the Federal Aviation Administration (FAA): Air Traffic Controller Furloughs and Congressional Response*. Congressional Research Service. May 7, 2013. https://www.fas.org/sgp/crs/misc/R43065.pdf/.

EUROCONTROL Performance Review Commission, FAA ATO Organization Systems Operations Services. 2010. *U.S./Europe Comparison of ATM-Related Operational Performance*. Washington, D.C.: EUROCONTROL.

European Aviation Safety Agency. 2015. *Advanced Notice of Proposed Amendment 201510*. Notice of Proposed Rule Making, European Aviation Safety Agency.

European Aviation Safety Agency. 2015. "Proposal to create common rules for operating drones in Europe." *Summary of the ANPA*. September. Accessed

October 15, 2015. https://www.easa.europa.eu/system/files/dfu/205933-01-EASA_Summary%20of%20the%20ANPA.pdf/.

Federal Aviation Administration. 2006. *Advisory Circular 120-92: Introduction to Safety Management Systems for Air Operators*. Advisory Circular, Washington, D.C.: Federal Aviation Administration.

Federal Aviation Administration. 2010. *Federal Register Volume 75, No. 194*. Washington, D.C.: BAE Systems.

Federal Aviation Administration. 2014. *Special Airworthiness Certification – Certification for Civil Operated Unmanned Aircraft Systems (UAS) and Optionally Piloted Aircraft (OPA)*. September 12. Accessed February 18, 2016. https://www.faa.gov/documentlibrary/media/order/8130.34c.pdf/.

Federal Aviation Administration. 2015. *Fact Sheet – Unmanned Aircraft Systems (UAS)*. February 12. Accessed August 10, 2015. https://www.faa.gov/news/fact_sheets/news_story.cfm?newsId=18297. http://www.faa.gov/aircraft/air_cert/airworthiness_certification/sp_awcert/experiment/sac/.

Florida v. Riley. 1989. 488 U.S. 445 (1989) (U.S. Supreme Court, January 23).

Frazier, Alan. 2012. "Law Enforcement Application of UAs: Burdens and Benefits." *AUVSI Power Point Presentation*. Washington, D.C.: AUVSI, March 3.

Government Accountability Office. 2012. *Unmanned Aircraft Systems – Measuring Progress and Addressing Potential Privacy Concerns Would Facilitate Integration into the National Airspace System*. GAO-12-981. September 18, 2012. http://www.gao.gov/assets/650/648348.pdf/.

Haddon, D.R. and C.J. Whittaker, 2004. *UK-CAA Policy for Light UAV Systems*. Policy Paper, London: UK Civil Aviation Authority.

Hallion, Richard and Michael Gorn. 2003. *On the Frontier: Experimental Flight at NASA Dryden*. Washington, D.C.: Smithsonian Books.

Hester v. United States. 1924. 265 U.S. 57 (1924) (U.S. Supreme Court).

Hsu, Jeremy. 2013. "Rise of the Drones: Unmanned Aircraft Sneak into the Arctic." *Livescience*. August 17. Accessed November 18, 2015. http://www.livescience.com/39194-drones-monitor-arctic.html/.

Idaho State Senate. 2013. "Senate Bill 1134: Unmanned Aircraft." Boise, Idaho: Legislative Services Office, July 1.

International Civil Aviation Authority. 1999. *International Civil Aviation Authority History*. Accessed May 13, 2015. http://www.icao.int/secretariat/Technical Cooperation/Pages/history.aspx/.

International Civil Aviation Authority. 1999. *International Civil Aviation Authority Home Page*. Accessed January 15, 2016. http://www.icao.int/about-icao/nclb/Pages/default.aspx/.

International Civil Aviation Organization. 2011. *ICAO Circular 328, Unmanned Aircraft Systems (UAS)*. Circular, Montreal, Canada: ICAO.

International Civil Aviation Organization. 2012. *International Civil Aviation Organization 2012 Safety Report*. Industry Safety Report, Montreal, Canada: International Civil Aviation Organization.

International Civil Aviation Organization. 2013. *Annex 19: International Standards and Recommended Practices*. Montreal, Canada: International Civil Aviation Organization.

Irish Aviation Authority, Safety Regulation Division. 2013. *Operation of Remotely Piloted Aircraft Systems in Irish Airspace*. Operations Advisory Memorandum, Dublin: IAA.

Jenkins, D. and Bijan Vasigh. 2013. *The Economic Impact of Unmanned Aircraft Systems Integration in the United States.* Industry Economic Impact Report, Washington, D.C.: Association for Unmanned Vehicle Systems International.

Khoza, Poppy. 2015. *Speech by the Director of Civil Aviation* Ms *Poppy Khoza at the Announcement of the Introduction of RPAS Regulations.* Speech, South Africa: SA Civil Aviation Authority.

Kyllo v. United States. 2001. 533 U.S. 27 (2001) (U.S. Supreme Court).

Ludwig, D., C. Andrews, J. Nienke, and C. Iaqui. 2007. *Safety Management Systems for Airports, Volume 1: Overview.* Airport Cooperative Research Program. file:///C:/Users/Wolf%20UAS%20LLC/Desktop/23163.pdf/.

McIninch, Thomas. 1994. *The Oxcart Story.* Accessed October 2013. https://www.cia.gov/library/center-for-the-study-of-intelligence/kent-csi/vol15no1/html/v15i1a01p_0001.htm/.

Mairena, Mario and Brett Davis. 2013. "Public Safety Use of UAS: A Legislative Update." *Unmanned Systems*, October 10: 21.

Merlin, Peter. 1974. "RPRVs – The First and Future Flights." *Astronautics and Aeronautics*, April: 26–42.

Merlin, Peter. 2001. *F-15 RPRV/SRV Flight Log.* Flight Log, Edwards, CA: NASA DFRC Historical Reference Collection.

Merlin, Peter. 2013. *Crash Course: Lessons Learned from Accidents Involving Remotely Piloted Aircraft.* Washington, D.C.: National Aeronautics and Space Administration.

MITRE. 1998. *Concept of Operations.* Accessed March 12, 2016. http://www.mitre.org/publications/systems-engineering-guide/se-lifecycle-building-blocks/concept-development/concept-of-operations/.

Montana State Legislature. 2013. "SB 196." *An Act Limiting the Use of Unmanned Aerial Vehicle by Law Enforcement; And Prohibiting the Use of Unlawfully Obtained Information as Evidence in Court.* Helena, Montana: Montana State Legislature, April 11.

Murphy, Darragh. 2014. "Game of Drones as Remote Pilots Ignore the Rules." *Irish Times.* August 14, 2014. http://www.irishtimes.com/life-and-style/people/game-of-drones-as-remote-pilots-ignore-the-rules-1.1891523/.

Murray, Patrick. 2012. "Monmouth University." *U.S. Supports Some Domestic Drone Use, but Public Registers Concern about Privacy.* June 12. Accessed January 8, 2015. http://www.monmouth.edu/assets/0/32212254770/32212254991/32212254992/32212254994/32212254995/30064771087/42e90ec6a27c40968b911ec51eca6000.pdf/.

Murray, Patrick. 2013. "Monmouth University." *National: U.S. Supports Unarmed Domestic Drones, but Public Prefers Requiring Court Orders First.* August 15. Accessed January 18, 2015. http://www.monmouth.edu/assets/0/32212254770/32212254991/32212254992/32212254994/32212254995/30064771087/409aecfb-3897-4360-8a05-03838ba69e46.pdf/.

National Conference of State Legislatures. 2013. *State Unmanned Aircraft Systems (UAS) Legislation.* Accessed 7/2/2015 http://www.ncsl.org/research/transportation/2013-state-unmanned-aircraft-systems-uas-legislation.aspx/.

National Transportation Safety Board. 2014. *Huerta v. Pirker.* Docket CP-217. March 6, 2014. http://www.ntsb.gov/legal/alj/Documents/Pirker-CP-217.pdf/.

Nicas, Jack, and Colum Murphy. 2014. "Wall Street Journal." *Who Builds the World's Most Popular Drones?* November 10. Accessed August 15, 2015. http://www.wsj.com/articles/who-builds-the-worlds-most-popular-drones-1415645659/.

Norris, G., and J. DiMascio. 2015. *Northrop Grumman Unveils Tern Tail-Sitter UAV.* Aerospace Daily and Defense Report. December 14. http://aviationweek.com/awindefense/northrop-grumman-unveils-tern-tail-sitter-uav/.

North Central Texas Regional General Aviation and Heliport System Plan. 2012. *Unmanned Aircraft Systems.* February 2012. Report. http://www.nctcog.org/trans/aviation/documents/Unmanned_Aircraft_Systems_Report_2_25_15_Update.pdf/.

Phelps, James, Harry Chiles, and William Peterson. 1974. *Report on F-15 RPRV Recovery Incident on July 10 1974.* Accident Investigation Report, Edwards, CA: NASA DFRC Historical Reference Collection.

Powers, M. 2016. *Short-term FAA extension may get pushback in the Senate. Politico: Morning Transportation.* March 15, 2016. http://www.politico.com/tipsheets/morning-transportation/2016/03/short-term-faa-extension-may-get-pushback-in-the-senate-fra-ruffles-feathers-with-crew-size-proposal-self-driving-cars-arrive-on-the-hill-literally-213211/.

Reed, Dale. 1980. *Flight Research Techniques Utilizing Remotely Piloted Aircraft Research Vehicles.* Technical Report AGARD-LS-108, Paper No. 8, Research Engineering, NASA Dryden Research Center: National Aeronautics and Space Administration.

Remote Control Aerial Platform Association 2014. *RCAPA Rebuttal to the FAA's Interpretation of the Special Rule for Model Aircraft.* July 4, 2014.http://rcapa.net/rebuttal-to-the-faas-interpretation/.

Sanders, S., and K. Downs. 2011. "Timeline of the WikiLeaks cable Release." *Washington Post,* 2011. http://www.washingtonpost.com/wp-srv/special/world/wikileaks-julian-assange-timeline/.

Skybrary. 2014. "European Aviation Safety Agency." *Skybrary.aero.* July 29. Accessed January 15, 2016. http://www.skybrary.aero/index.php/European_Aviation_Safety_Agency_(EASA)/.

Spin Research Vehicle Project. 1980. *Project Document OPD 80-67, Spin Research Vehicle Shape Project.* Project Document, Edwards, CA: NASA DFRC Historical Reference Collection.

Subbaraman, Nidhi. 2013. "Drones over America: How unmanned fliers are already helping cops." *NBCNews.com.* March 30. Accessed February 2, 2014. http://www.nbcnews.com/technology/drones-over-america-how-unmanned-fliers-are-already-helping-cops-1C9135554/.

Szoldra, P. 2014. "SNOWDEN: Here's Everything We've Learned in One Year of Unprecedented Top-Secret Leaks." *Business Insider.* June 7, 2014.

Teal Group. 2014. *Worldwide UAV Market Study Report.* Market Report, Teal Group.

The European Commission. 2016. *Official Journal of the European Union. Commission_Regulation_EU_4_2016.* January 6. Accessed March 18, 2016. http://www.caa.bg/upload/docs/COMMISSION_REGULATION__EU__4_2016.pdf/.

United Arab Emirates General Aviation Authority. 2015. *UAS Registration.* December 16. Accessed March 18, 2016. https://www.gcaa.gov.ae/en/pages/UASRegistration.aspx/.

U.S. Congress. 2012. "H.R. 658 (112th): FAA Modernization and Reform Act of 2012." Washington, D.C.: Federal Register, February 14.

U.S. Department of Transportation. 1981. Federal Aviation Administration. Advisory Circular 91—57. June 9, 1981. https://www.faa.gov/documentLibrary/media/Advisory_Circular/91-57.pdf/.

U.S. Department of Transportation. 2009. "Safety Management System (SMS) Aviation Rulemaking Committee Order 1110.152." Washington, DC. 02/12/2009. https://www.faa.gov/documentLibrary/media/Order/1110.152.pdf/.

United States Congress. 1958. "Federal Aviation Act of 1958." *Public Law 85-726.* Washington, D.C.: Federal Register, August 28.

Virginia Commonwealth House of Delegates. 2013. "House Bill 2012 Drones; Moratorium on use of unmanned aircraft systems by state or local government department, etc." Richmond, VA: Virginia General Assembly, January 9.

Walker, John. 2010. *Contributing Stakeholders: RTCA SC-203. 2010- 2011 UAS Yearbook – UAS: The Global Perspective.* © Blyenburgh & Co., page 71/214. http://uvs-info.com/phocadownload/05_3b_2010/P071-072_RTCA-SC203_John-Walker.pdf/.

Walls, Bennett. 2014. *Civilian Drones, Privacy, and the Federal-State-Balance.* Research Report & Policy Memo, The Brookings Institution, 15–20.

Yamaha Motor Australia. 2013. *RMAX Type II G / Type II.* Accessed March 18, 2016. http://rmax.yamaha-motor.com.au/features/.

Yamaha Motor Australia. 2013. *Yamaha RMAX Type II G/Type II.* Accessed March 18, 2016. http://rmax.yamaha-motor.com.au/history/.

Index

Page numbers in **bold** denote figures and page numbers in *italics* denote tables.

Printed in the United States
by Baker & Taylor Publisher Services